HEATHER!

HEATHER!

An Unabashed, Unauthorized Celebration of All Things Locklear

JODIE GOULD

A CITADEL PRESS BOOK
PUBLISHED BY CAROL PUBLISHING GROUP

A Citadel Press Book

Published by Carol Publishing Group

Citadel Press is a registered trademark of Carol Communications, Inc.

Editorial Offices: 600 Madison Avenue, New York, N.Y. 10022

Sales and Distribution Offices: 120 Enterprise Avenue, Secaucus, N.J. 07094

In Canada: Canadian Manda Group, One Atlantic Avenue, Suite 105, Toronto, Ontario M6K 3E7

Queries regarding rights and permissions should be addressed to Carol Publishing Group, 600 Madison Avenue, New York, N.Y. 10022

Carol Publishing Group books are available at special discounts for bulk purchases, sales promotion, fund-raising, or educational purposes. Special editions can be created to specifications. For details, contact: Special Sales Department, Carol Publishing Group, 120 Enterprise Avenue, Secaucus, N.J. 07094.

Manufactured in the United States of America

10 9 8 7 6 5 4 3 2 1

Library of Congress Cataloging-in-Publication Data

Gould, Jodie.

    Heather! : an unabashed, unauthorized celebration of all things Locklear / Jodie Gould.

      p. cm.

    "A Citadel Press book."

    ISBN 0-8065-1668-2 (pbk.)

    1. Locklear, Heather—Miscellanea. I. Title.

PN2287.L57G68 1995

791.45'092—dc20   95-9534

  [B]   CIP

Dedication

To my husband, Bob, with love. May our lives together be
nothing like an episode of *Melrose Place*.

Acknowledgments

My sincere thanks and gratitude: to Ben Petrone for recommending me for this project and to my editor, Kevin McDonough, for allowing me to run with his inspired idea. To Diane Mancher, Melinda Mullin (of One Potata), and Catherine Dold for their support and ever vigilant Heather watch. To Phil Mattera of the Writers Union for his guidance and Linda Konner of ASJA for hers. To Beryl Meyer, Cheryl Kahn, and Sherry Cremona for their referrals, and, finally, to Hillary Schupf and Fred Gioffre for their *Melrose* mania.

Behind the Scenes at Melrose Place

Standing on the set of *Melrose*, Heather practices her lines for one of the thirty-two episodes that will be shot this year. "How dare you?" she says, scowling. "How *dare* you!" She's dressed in a tan suit with a miniskirt that hugs her bare thighs. It's an outfit which, in the real world of business, might be seen as an invitation for sexual harassment.

"The nerve!" she hisses.

"How dare you!"

The set is located in the hills of Santa Clarita, about fifteen miles north of Los Angeles. This is where Heather spends most of her time, rising before dawn to arrive on the set by 7 A.M.

Hours later, when she breaks for lunch, she goes into her trailer to change into more comfortable garb—her signature blue jeans with a tear under the back pocket, just large enough to reveal a glimpse of the boxer shorts underneath.

Her trailer is filled with scented candles, more Amanda suits, and some slinky dresses designed by Richard Tyler. Scattered on the dressing table is hair root spray, a picture of Heather with her dad, and lysine for cold sores. Her refrigerator houses some sadly neglected chicken take-out and a bottle of champagne from a fan.

She throws on a plaid workshirt, worn on the outside to conceal the hole in her pants, and steps into her shiny black

Opposite: "You can't get too deep and go, 'Oh great, is this what life is about?'"

> **(Wayne and Garth spot Heather backstage at an Aerosmith concert)**
> **WAYNE:** Garth, it's Heather Locklear! (*Celestial music*) She's signaling to us. There *is* a God!
> **GARTH:** (*Reverently*) Heather be thy name.

Mercedes. She casually tosses a black bra that is draped over the front seat into the back before speeding off to the restaurant.

An admitted food hound, "I have a real fast metabolism," Heather orders an enormous plate of pasta and sausage and a large salad with cheese. Unlike other actresses and models for whom food is the enemy, Heather heartily cleans her plate.

When she returns to the set, the crew gathers around the infamous apartment complex while Heather rushes off to wardrobe. She reappears, script in hand, wearing the same tan suit she wore that morning.

She and Daphne Zuniga, who plays Jo, rehearse a scene in which they are fighting over (who else?) Jake. Every so often a stylist comes over to powder a nose or primp hair. The scene is shot without a hitch and, afterward, Heather makes a bee-line for her trailer to prepare for another scene. She does not go home until late that evening.

Heather said the long hours spent parroting lines that can only be characterized as high soap drama distract her from the existential thoughts that sometimes creep into her consciousness.

"I think when you don't have a goal you question: 'What is this about? What are things for?'" she mused between sips of Evian. "At least when you're working, you don't have time to ponder all that. You can't get too deep and go, 'Oh great, is this what life is about?'"

For now, that goal is to be Amanda Woodward, and to inhabit a strange universe with eight young and beautiful people whose lives intersect like the lines of a dysfunctional Spirograph.

It means going to the occasional press party, like the one thrown by the Fox Network at the Los Angeles Hard Rock Cafe. Heather arrives fashionably late in a white T-shirt and black jumper, her luxurious blond locks piled into a loose bun. The celebrity journalists immediately swarm, armed with notebooks, cameras, and tape recorders.

Opposite: Melrose Place: Amanda (Heather Locklear) gets close to Jake (Grant Show).

"We have such a great cast and a fun storyline," Heather tells one reporter. She spots a fellow cast member across the room and sticks her tongue out playfully. She graciously signs autographs and gives Josie Bissett (Jane) a hug. A young fan gushes to a TV crew filming the Event: "When I told my dad I was going to see Heather Locklear, he said, 'If you don't get me her autograph I'm going to kill you.'"

"My family is real normal and close."

The media madness is interrupted by a Hard Rock employee, who introduces the cast as they jog onto the stage like players at the Super Bowl. As the show's star quarterback, Heather is the last to be announced. The fans go wild and the people at Fox eagerly lap up the excitement. The crowd screams, "Mondays are a bitch" for a sound bite, and the actors line up for one last photo op.

The party is over, and Heather is ushered back into her limo with an armful of Hard Rock jackets and other promotional goodies.

With *Melrose* headed for its fourth season in '95, Heather's future is, for the time being, secure. Far from an overnight success, Heather has been an actress for more than a decade; she has worked hard to get to the top, where she currently reigns as the nineties' Queen of TV.

In the last two years, she's been profiled in countless national magazines, such as *Vanity Fair, Details, Mademoiselle,* and *New Woman.* She did a dry-eyed interview with Barbara Walters, and boosted the ratings of *Saturday Night Live* by being a guest host. She's received every conceivable media accolade, from "Most Beautiful," "Most Fascinating," and "Most Lovable," to "Most Influential Female Body."

The long hours, the perseverance, the refusal to be dismissed as the flavor of the week, have finally paid off. After more than a decade in show business, Heather is at the top of her game. "This year I've worked the hardest," she said recently, "and probably been the happiest. . . . The critics figured I'd be gone by now, just another blonde. But I never thought I'd be a flash. The best revenge is sticking around."

Childhood

Heather Dean Locklear was born on September 25, 1961, at the UCLA Medical Center. A bona fide Valley Girl right down to her dark roots, Heather was raised in a large one-story Tudor home in Canoga Park, a middle-class suburb in the San Fernando Valley. When she was six, the family moved to nearby Westlake, just twenty minutes from downtown Hollywood.

Heather's father, Bill, now heads the career placement office at UCLA, where he was previously dean of admissions. A former colonel in the Marine Corps, Heather's conservative dad raised his children to believe in the traditional values of God and country.

When her parents threatened to spank her in front of a roomful of people, Heather vehemently protested. "I never got spanked again," she said.

Diane Locklear, from whom Heather inherited her blond hair and dazzling blue eyes, started out as an administrative assistant in the postproduction office at the Disney studios. Later she was promoted to film editor and is now in the casting department.

Unlike Amanda's dead-beat dad and model-hawking mom, Heather credits her real-life parents with providing a happy and nurturing environment. She remembers crawling into her parents' bedroom as a toddler for a comforting hug whenever she had a nightmare. "I had such a good childhood," she said. "My family is real normal and close."

The fact that Heather's parents stressed academics over performing helped keep Heather and her siblings from succumbing too quickly to the lure of Hollywood. Heather said she had always dreamed of being a helicopter pilot when she grew up—not a model or actress. "I must have seen something on television and thought it looked neat," she explained. "Mom and Dad pushed us to study hard and get somewhere."

And the Locklear children got the message all right; all four siblings went on to college (although Heather dropped out in her sophomore year). Her oldest sister, Laurie, works for a doctor; her brother, Mark, whom she shared a room with until she was eleven, is an appraiser; and Colleen does wardrobe for Yanni.

Every summer the Locklears would take the kids to a rented cabin in Lake Arrowhead, California, one hundred miles east of Los Angeles. Heather has fond memories of water-skiing behind boats that were too slow to pull the adults out of the water. Every winter, the family would make a trip to the nearby Santa's Village amusement park, where one day Heather got a cut on her lip when she was hit by an icy snowball. She loved the place so much that she would later buy the cabin to share with her family, friends, agent, manager, and, eventually, husbands.

Religion also played a major role in the Locklear household. Heather regularly attended the First Baptist Church of Canoga Park and, when the family moved, the United Methodist Church in Westlake. Raised to honor her mother and father, the ever dutiful daughter did "whatever my parents said."

It wasn't until the age of six that Heather first rebelled. When her parents threatened to spank her in front of a roomful of people, Heather vehemently protested. She managed to convince her parents to forgo the humiliating punishment. "I never got spanked again," she said.

Heather said she had always dreamed of being a helicopter pilot when she grew up—not a model or actress.

High School: The Awkward Years

The ugly duckling who grows into a startling beauty is a cliché, but that's exactly how Heather describes her awkward adolescence. Seeing her today, with her wholesome, sun-drenched good looks, one might assume that she was the head cheerleader or homecoming queen. The truth is, Heather was neither the best student nor the most popular girl at Newbury Park High School.

"I love tacos with all the fake cheese."

"In high school I was nothing," she said candidly. "The closest I ever came to [getting] somewhere in high school was when I tried out for cheerleader. But I didn't make the squad. That rejection took me a long time to get over."

The disappointed teen joined the chorus instead. But singing did little to help Heather's flagging self-confidence. Ashamed of her scrawny physique and acne-plagued skin, Heather became increasingly withdrawn. She wore sweatshirts to school, even on the hottest days, "to hide my bony arms and knobby elbows."

It is an image of herself that she still finds difficult to shake. "When I look in the mirror, I see the girl I was growing up, with braces, crooked teeth, a baby face, and a skinny body."

She remembers how a few of the kids in school would tease her about being flat-chested. She dealt with the taunts by laughing right along with them. Her strategy seemed to work. "I wanted them to know that I knew I was flat-chested," she said. "I mean, like, so what?" So then it would be like, 'Oh, isn't she funny? She's laughing!' "

But underneath, the incidents made her feel even more uncomfortable socially. "I was always shy," she recalled. "Somebody else had to start the conversation or make the first move." She was so bashful around people, that she once opted to take an F rather than deliver a monologue in front of the class. "My heart pounded so hard you could see my blouse move."

Despite the struggle with her appearance and social skills, Heather managed to meet a boy in high school whom she dated for several years. "We broke up just a few months before the senior prom," she recalled. Not wanting to miss the big event, the two reunited once more on prom night.

She briefly joined the drama club, hoping it would help to

cure her debilitating shyness. She discovered that her fear of performing would disappear whenever she pretended to be someone else. "I was always okay playing a part, but when I had to be myself—making a speech, for instance—I went to pieces. Being someone else is so much easier."

She resisted the idea of going into acting. Instead she would go to college to study psychology.

From College to Commercials to Camera

In 1979, Heather enrolled at UCLA as a psych major, just as she had planned. By this time, the awkward adolescent had blossomed into a cute and curvaceous coed. She briefly went to modeling school, only to discover that at five-feet-five, she was too short to walk the runway. Instead, her father suggested that she pose for the university's BearWear clothing catalog, for which she did the first of what would be many cover shoots.

Although her parents lived nearby, she opted to live in a dorm. After all, she could visit her dad every day at the admissions office on campus.

The now beautiful Heather, who was having trouble deciding between psychology and physical education, had to be coaxed out of her shell by friends. "I thought I'd just float along in life. I didn't think I was going to have a career." But her friends could see in her what she hadn't yet discovered about herself—she had star quality.

"When my friends suggested I give acting a try, I had to muster up as much courage as I could," she said. She remembered how horrible she felt in high school when she didn't make the cheerleading squad, and she wasn't sure if she could

take the rejection; but she also knew how great it felt to jump into another person's skin. Besides, she could use the money.

If it didn't work out, she told herself, she could always become a psychologist. So she signed up for a commercial workshop at the university's prestigious drama department. There the freshman was "discovered" by a visiting talent scout from Wilhelmina Artists, one of the largest modeling agencies in Los Angeles.

Said her longtime acting coach Howard Fine: "People always make the mistake of underestimating Heather. She can hold the stage—and the camera—with anyone."

The agency started her on modeling jobs for print catalogs;

"Make them stop! Please make them stop!"

within months, she was doing a spate of commercials for Tame creme rinse and STP motor oil and other products. The assignments were simple. Show off your gams and your gums. And, for a while, the scantily clad Heather did nothing but pose and smile.

"I did not utter a single word," Heather recalled of her early commercials. She braided her hair for Coca-Cola; flipped that same head of hair for Tame; and winked coquettishly at actor James Garner for Polaroid. Later she was allowed to extoll the virtues of milk or coo "Sea and Ski me" in her best impression

Opposite: For a while, the scantily clad Heather did nothing but pose and smile.

of a beach-blanket bimbo.

Her classmates were thrilled, calling her up every time they spotted her on television. Her parents were also proud of their daughter, but deeply disappointed when she told them that she would be dropping out her sophomore year to become a full-time actress. "I had my mother tell my father, since I knew he wouldn't be too pleased about it," she said.

Heather wanted to finish college, but she found it impossible to juggle her schoolwork and the demands of her budding show business career. She made the decision to leave school after staying up one night until 5 A.M. to complete a paper. "I never found out what I got on that paper," she said. "I didn't care."

Free to devote all her time to auditions and call-backs, Heather quickly landed her first TV role on the show *CHiPs,* where she played a hostage rescued by the teenage heartthrob Erik Estrada. She said she will never forget her first dramatic lines for television: "Make them stop! Please make them stop!"

Continuing with the hostage theme, she appeared on a show called *240-Robert* with the hunky Mark Harmon. After that, she played other bite-size roles on the *Beverly Hillbillies Special* and as Willie Aame's love interest in *Eight Is Enough.* Blink and you missed her.

One of her first big breaks came in the form of a TV movie called *Twirl,* where she finally got to trumpet teen spirit as a high school baton twirler.

"She was delightful," recalled Bonnie Forbes, who produced the two-hour movie for NBC. "She was young, funny, and obviously talented. She was in the film with Erin Moran from *Happy Days,* and Erin was totally out of control. She drove her Corvette into a plate-glass window during the filming. Heather, by contrast, was basically your typical Hollywood starlet—filled with dreams, hopes, and aspirations."

Her TV movie debut caught the eye of mega-producer Aaron Spelling, which led to larger roles on *The Love Boat* and *Fantasy Island.* They would open up the door to the show that would launch her career as a small-screen icon. In 1981, Heather answered a casting call for another Spelling production. It was for a new TV series called *Dynasty.*

Opposite: Howard Fine: "People always make the mistake of under-estimating Heather."

Sammy Jo: TV's Princess of Nasty

Heather's first great television role was in *Dynasty*, playing flashy, trashy Sammy Jo, the fortune-seeking precursor to Amanda Woodward. It was the role that would define Heather as the actress born to play the princess of nasty.

The prime-time soap about Denver's obscenely rich Carrington clan (originally named *Oil*) debuted on January 12, 1981. Heather would spend eight years as the wife of Blake Carrington's black-sheep son Steven. And much like *Melrose*, *Dynasty* was not an instant critical success.

"It's a mighty low-grade crude that comes oozing out of the tube in *Dynasty*," Tom Buckley of the *New York Times* wrote of the series' three-hour premiere. "An embarrassingly obvious knockoff of *Dallas*. . . . not one of the characters had a moment of believability in the endless opening installment."

Buckley later added: "Stringent budgeting is apparent throughout the production, from the one-take shots that scarcely seem to have been directed at all to an unconvincing oil-well fire and the obviously pulled punches in the fight sequences."

Even the tabloids yawned. "Off to a dull start, *Dynasty's* destiny is hard to predict," wrote Kay Gardella of the *New York Post*. "Some improvement is possible as the weeks roll along. If not, the Carringtons' dynasty will surely come to an end."

Still, what *Dynasty* lacked in believability, it made up for with high-camp glitz and glamour. The show eventually caught on with the prime-time soap lovers, pulling in a whopping 100 million viewers in seventy-eight countries. It was a major career booster not just for Heather, but for many of the cast members

Opposite: Sammy Jo (Heather) and the "first" Steven (Al Corley).

Dynasty was a full-fledged, high-camp prime-time soap that symbolized the zeitgeist of the eighties in the same way that *Melrose* is a benchmark of the more politically polarized Clinton/Gingrich nineties. About mid-decade, critic at large Stephen Schiff deconstructed *Dynasty* for *Vanity Fair,* the period's favorite periodical:

"The soap opera is a populist form, but *Dynasty's* chichi creates an antipopulist setting. And America has never been less populist than it has been under Ronald Reagan. No one wants to be a grimy prole in a society that offers no rewards to grimy proles—not even the assumption of virtue. Under the tenets of supply-side economics, '80s America not only kowtows to the rich, but holds them up as a moral standard. It is they who, given money enough and tax breaks, will kindly allow their property to trickle down to the rest of us. Thereby saving the American economy and Life as We Know It."

John James, Terri Garber, Heather, and Jack Coleman.

"*I'm no Madonna.*"

who would become household names.

John Forsythe played the family patriarch, Blake Carrington; Linda Evans portrayed his sadly misunderstood second wife, Krystle; and TV's reigning bitch diva and glam queen, Joan Collins, played Blake's ex-wife Alexis.

"We decided to add a young person to the cast, a fun character who could eat hamburgers and slide down banisters," explained producer Elaine Rich of the show's decision to bring in Sammy Jo. They needed someone to play the younger, fair-haired niece of Linda Evans. Someone who looked like an angel but had a cold heart and a bad-girl reputation. The part was tailor-made for Heather.

The tortuous storyline went something like this: Blake Carrington ran his oil company from an opulent forty-eight-room mansion in Denver. When the series began, his business was on the brink of disaster because Mideast revolutionaries had stolen his tankers.

Blake's beautiful but unhappy wife, Krystle, whom he wooed and won when she was a secretary, is virtually ignored by the powerful patriarch. Krystle's perennial slugfest with the older but equally beautiful Alexis, who was intent on securing her place in the Carrington dynasty, was one of the series' highlights.

Sammy Jo was also a favorite among *Dynasty*'s remarkably long list of characters. She was left with the Carringtons by her father, Charles (Rock Hudson), and almost immediately made the move on their youngest son, Steve. Eager to get her manicured hands onto the Carrington fortune, she marries Steve before the end of the first season.

Sammy Jo joined forces with the evil producer Joel in a scheme to kidnap Krystle and substitute a look-alike actress named Rita. Remarkably, Blake didn't seem to notice the difference, even in bed. Sammy Jo jilted her husband, blackmailed her mother-in-law, Alexis, and abandoned her son Danny to chase after a career in modeling.

The competition for the juicy role of Sammy Jo was intense. Heather auditioned with 450 other hopeful ingenues, and was one of only four women asked to do a screen test. When she learned that she had gotten the job, she was desperate to share the good news.

"I was moving out of my college apartment," Heather recalled, "and there was no one there to tell. No one. Dad was in a meeting. I remember going downstairs to find someone— the mailman, even. And I wondered what people would think, like my first-grade teacher. I wondered, 'Were people going to change toward me? Was I going to change toward them?'"

The answer, inevitably, was yes. Shortly afterward, Heather split with the UCLA student she had been seeing for some time. Like it or not, she was no longer just another struggling young actress. "I guess the breakup was caused by a mixture of everything," she said in retrospect. "I think his ego was involved."

Heather was so concerned about how fame might change her that she made a solemn vow that night. "I prayed that if I got a

Did you know that oil baron Blake Carrington rose from humble beginnings as a soda jerk at a Pennsylvania diner called Annie's Eats? And that the fictitious Denver company also had offices in New York near Wall Street? Or that only Eastern-educated WASPs were allowed to sit on its esteemed board. You might also like to know that this information came from a 1985 book called *Dynasty: The Authorized Biography of the Carringtons* by Esther Shapiro. Ms. Shapiro is the non-WASPy cocreator of the once-popular series.

big head or got too big for my britches, something would happen to me so I couldn't work anymore."

To make sure she would spend her newfound money wisely, Heather handed over all of her paychecks to her accountant, asking that he apportion a certain amount each week to her as an allowance.

In addition to exercising such fiscal self-control, Heather's acute shyness and natural humility acted as built-in mechanisms against star tripping.

"I was only twenty and I got really scared," she recalled. "I thought, 'Oh my God, I'm not going to be able to go to the movies anymore, I'm going to have to wear dark glasses.'" She paused before adding ruefully. "And it was so sad, because I *never* had to wear dark glasses. I'm no Madonna."

Maybe, but she was certainly a major player in the TV big leagues. Soon she became far too busy trying to learn her craft to worry about the price of celebrity. She will never forget how terrified she was her first day on the *Dynasty* set. "I was a wreck," she said. "I was all-around nervous."

In fact, she became so agitated that she once mistook Joan Collins for Linda Evans. She ran up to Collins asking, "Are you my aunt Krystle?" In another scene with Collins, her jittery nerves made it difficult to walk down the stairs, slip on her pumps, and speak her lines at the same time. "My foot was shaking so much I couldn't get the shoe on. . . ."

"What are you sup-posed to do?" she asked the director soberly. "Stutter? Slobber? I've never been drunk."

Nevertheless, viewers took notice of the gorgeous newcomer, and she quickly developed a following. She was the hot new discovery of the eighties. But she knew she would have to work even harder to stay in the public eye.

On one of her rare days off, she flew three thousand miles to appear at a decidedly unglamorous auto show in Hartford, Connecticut. For eight hours, she sat on the stage surrounded by cars and admirers, graciously signing autographs. The rock music was deafening, the food was awful, and the videos on the huge screen behind her were out of focus.

When an incredulous reporter asked her why she had accepted such a low-profile gig, she responded: "Once they meet you, they're your loyal fans. They'll watch you forever."

Although the Nielsen families were watching, not everyone at *Dynasty* was so enamored with the neophyte actress. Producer Elaine Rich acknowledged that Heather was "everything we hoped for, with a warmth and appeal that goes beyond her being pretty." But her inexperience soon showed like a black slip beneath a beautiful white dress.

"I walked on the set one day, and she was doing a scene where she had to come through a door, pause, and then begin speaking," Rich recalled. "She came through the door all right,

Opposite: Sammy Jo between two hunks. How unusual!

BLAKE CARRINGTON:
John Forsythe

KRYSTLE JENNINGS CARRINGTON:
Linda Evans

ALEXIS CARRINGTON COLBY:
Joan Collins

SAMMY JO DEAN: (1981–1989):
Heather Locklear

FALLON CARRINGTON COLBY
(1981–84):
Pamela Sue Martin

FALLON CARRINGTON COLBY
(1985, 1987–89)
Emma Samms

STEVEN CARRINGTON
(1981–1982):
Al Corley

STEVEN CARRINGTON
(1982–1988): Jack Coleman

ADAM CARRINGTON/MICHAEL
TORRANCE (1982–1989):
Gordon Thomson

CECIL COLBY (1981–82):
Lloyd Bochner

JEFF COLBY (1981–85;
1987–89):
John James

CLAUDIA BLAISDEL (1981–86):
Pamela Bellwood

MATTHEW BLAISDEL (1981):
Bo Hopkins

LINDSAY BLAISDEL (1981): Katy
Kurtzman

WALTER LANDERSHIM (1981):
Dale Robertson

JOSEPH ANDERS (1981–83):
Lee Bergere

KIRBY (1982–84):
Kathleen Beller

ANDREW LAIRD (1981–84):
Peter Mark Richman

MICHAEL CULHANE (1981;
1986–87): Wayne Northrop

DR. NICK TOSCANNI (1981–82):
James Farentino

MARK JENNINGS (1982–84):
Geoffrey Scott

CONGRESSMAN NEAL MCVANE
(1982–84; 1987):
Paul Burke

TRACY KENDALL (1983–84):
Deborah Adair

FARNSWORTH "DEX" DEXTER
(1983–89):
Michael Nader

PETER DE VILBIS (1983–84):
Helmut Berger

AMANDA CARRINGTON
(1984–86):
Catherine Oxenberg

AMANDA CARRINGTON
(1986–87): Karen Cellini

DOMINIQUE DEVERAUZ
(1984–87):
Diahann Carroll

GORDON WALES (1984–88):
James Sutorius

LUKE FULLER (1984–85):
William Campbell

NICOLE SIMPSON (1984–85):
Susan Scannell

DANIEL REECE (1984–1985):
Rock Hudson

CHARLES (1984–85):
George DiCenzo

LADY ASHLEY MITCHELL (1985):
Ali McGraw

DANNY CARRINGTON (1985–88):
Jameson Sampley

JOEL ABRIGORE (1985–86):
George Hamilton

GARRETT BOYDSON (1985–86):
Ken Howard

KING GALEN (1985–86):
Joel Fabiani

PRINCE MICHAEL (1985–86):
Michael Praed

SENATOR BUCK FALLMONT (1986–87):
Richard Anderson

EMILY FALLMONT (1986):
Pat Crowley

CLAY FALLMONT (1986–87):
Ted McGinley

BEN CARRINGTON (1986–87):
Christopher Cazenone

JACKIE DEVERAUX (1986–87):
Troy Beyer

CARESS MORELL (1986):
Kate O'Mara

DANA WARING CARRINGTON (1986–88): Leann Hanley

NICK KIMBALL (1986–87):
Richard Lawson

LESLIE CARRINGTON (1987–88):
Terri Garber

SEAN ROWAN (1987–88):
James Healey

KRYSTINA CARRINGTON (1987–89):
Jessica Player

SARAH CURTIS (1987):
Cassie Yates

KAREN ATKINSON (1987–88)
Stephanie Dunnham

SABLE COLBY (1988–89)
Stephanie Beacham

SGT. JOHNNY ZORELLI (1988–89):
Ray Abruzzo

CLAIRE TENNYSON (1988):
Stella Hall

VIRGINIA METHENY (1988–89):
Liza Morrow

CAPT. WILLIAM HANDLER (1988–89):
John Brandon

RUDY RICHARDS (1988–89):
Lou Beatty Jr.

MONICA COLBY (1989):
Tracy Scoggins

FATHER TANNER MCBRIDE (1989): Kevin Bernhardt

but couldn't seem to pause. I said, 'Oh my God! Have her learn to count to three!'" Heather also had a few problems with her as yet untrained voice. "Send her to a voice coach to learn to lower that screech a couple of octaves," Rich demanded.

Humiliations such as these helped keep Heather humble, according to others who worked with her. Chuck Ashman, then a merchandising and marketing executive for *Dynasty*-related products, said he would have to go through a coterie of PR types, personal managers, assistants, boyfriends, and body-guards to get to Joan Collins, Linda Evans, or Catherine Oxenberg. Not so with Heather.

"Heather always acted like we were doing her a favor and would be the first to arrive and last to leave at every event," Ashman recalled. "And her fans knew it. She typified the very best in star behavior, and that has never changed."

Determined to prove that she was more than another pretty face, Heather enrolled in acting and voice classes to work on her technique. "I have a long way to go," she conceded at the time, "but that's part of the fun of it, seeing yourself improve. And I am trying to improve myself. I am *not* just taking a ride."

With time and practice, Heather's acting improved. Even her formidable costars commented on her changing status. "The child has turned into a damn fine actress," Linda Evans remarked. And Heather's mentor of meanness, Joan Collins, agreed: "The kid's a real pro."

But Heather knew she would have to convince the audience, as well as the industry, that inside that sweet, California dream-boat was a bad girl screaming to come out. Sammy Jo was a role that Heather would grow into with time.

"When Sammy Jo first came on the air, I wasn't crazy about her personality," she said. "She was not a nice girl. She eventually became more responsible and a good mother. But it was more fun to play when she was bad."

And where a more seasoned actor could cull from a lifetime of experience to play her character, the unworldly Heather often felt as if she was fishing in a dry lake. In those days, Heather was such a straight arrow that she didn't even know how to act drunk. "What are you supposed to do?" she asked the director soberly. "Stutter? Slobber? I've never been drunk."

Heather being held by Steven Shortridge on the *Dynasty* reunion

She had no trouble, however, performing her steamy bedroom scenes with Ted McGinley, who played Sammy Jo's other husband, Clay Fallmont. "We try to make our love scenes together as real as possible," McGinley once said. "It helps if you don't have garlic the night before," Heather added.

Despite the realism of the lovemaking, there were no off-screen romances between Heather and any of *Dynasty's* leading men. Getting involved with coworkers, she said at the time, is "dangerous and uncomfortable."

As it happened, Heather would later get the chance to play nice as well as vice. After twelve episodes of *Dynasty*, Sammy Jo suddenly vanished—and so did Heather's job. She immediately searched for another role and was offered the part as goody-goody rookie cop Stacy Sheridan on *T. J. Hooker*.

After a few months on *Hooker*, the *Dynasty* writers wanted Sammy Jo to return to her husband with an infant son in her arms. But there was one minor problem. Actor Al Corley was no longer interested in playing the role of the resurrected Steve Carrington.

No big whoop for dedicated soap watchers, who are more than happy to suspend their disbelief for the sake of a juicy

"I prayed that if I got a big head or got too big for my britches, something would happen to me so I couldn't work anymore."

The Carrington mansion was actually the Filoli estate just south of San Francisco.

*John Forsythe was not the first choice to play Blake Carrington. George Peppard had been hired for the pilot, but he bolted after a fight with executives over how the part should be played.

*Alexis's full name: Alexis Morell Carrington Colby Dexter Rowan

*Dynasty's weekly wardrobe budget of $10,000 was the highest in TV.

*In 1983, former president Gerald Ford and his wife Betty appeared in a Dynasty episode, as did former secretary of state Henry Kissinger.

story line. "It's that old Saturday matinee *Flash Gordon* syndrome transferred to adult audiences," observed one TV columnist. "Leave 'em on the edge of their seats—and they'll come running back for more . . ."

And that's precisely what the *Dynasty* producers did. First they hired the handsome Jack Coleman to fill in. Then they conjured up an explosion at the oil plant, adding a little plastic surgery to explain the sudden change of face.

Meanwhile Heather was already engaged as the squeaky-clean Stacy. Again, the solution was simple. Since both shows came under the Aaron Spelling umbrella, and Stacy was still a minor character, Heather agreed to juggle her schedule so she could play both parts simultaneously.

"I have more fun playing Sammy Jo because I do anything I want with her," Heather said of her dual roles back in 1983. "She's so conniving and mean. She's wacky and not like me at all. But Stacy is an upstanding young woman and much more like I am."

If America didn't know the name Heather Locklear before, it sure would now. In addition to her ubiquitous appearances on TV, she was asked to model summerwear for the cover of *Los Angeles* magazine and sexy swimwear on the cover of *US*. Everywhere you looked, you saw Heather.

As Sammy Jo, Heather was a bitch-in-training to then-reigning diva Joan Collins. How does Heather's *Melrose* character Amanda compare with *Dynasty's* Alexis when viewed side by side?

AMANDA: Wears thigh-grabbing, attention-getting suits with comfortable but sexy shoes. She's got a head for business, and a bod for getting busy.

ALEXIS: Wore cleavage-revealing, attention-getting broadshouldered suits with uncomfortable spiked heels. She had a head for business, and was the busiest of all bodies.

AMANDA: Likes younger men.

ALEXIS: Marries a younger man.

AMANDA: A perfect bitch, plots against blond rival Alison. Constantly planning her next maneuver to THE HEAD OF D&D.

ALEXIS: A perfect bitch, plots against blond rival Krystle. Constantly planning her next maneuver to the head of the Carrington family.

AMANDA: Appears in court as defendant in sexual harassment case against ex-employee.

ALEXIS: Appears in court as witness for the prosecution against her ex-husband Blake.

AMANDA: Thanks to Amanda, Melrose Mondays have become a social ritual for millions of Americans in the nineties.

ALEXIS: Thanks to Alexis, "Dinner and Dynasty" was a fixture of social life for millions of Americans in the eighties. Tapes of the epic catfights between Alexis and Krystle (such as the tumble down a muddy hill) were played each night at many gay bars.

AMANDA: Shows that women over thirty are still hot.

ALEXIS: Showed that women over forty can still be hot.

ALEXIS TO A PREGNANT KRYSTLE: "Oh, Krystle, even *worms* procreate."

AMANDA TO ALISON: "Cross me again, and you'll have that proverbial wish that you'd never been born."

Beam Me Up, T. J.

Between 1982 and 1986, Heather would often spend three days a week filming *Hooker*, the ironically named and highly implausible cop show starring *Star Trek*'s William Shatner. On the days when she was needed on both shows, she would race from one set to another for a two-minute scene here and a ten-minute scene there.

Heather did her double duty like a, well, trooper. Of course, it didn't hurt that she could sleepwalk through her role as Stacy, and that she was pulling in $20,000 an episode for *Dynasty* alone.

The show's story line revolved around Sergeant Hooker, who gave up his detective shield and civilian clothes for a job with the uniformed police force. The reason: that's where he was needed. He was assigned to the Academy Precinct of the "LAPD," where he could play mentor to trainees like Stacy and rookie boy scouts like his partner, Officer Vince Romano (Adrian Zmed).

Unlike the evil-spinning Carrington clan, Hooker stood for traditional values. Captain Sheridan (Richard Herd) was Stacy's by-the-book father, and T. J.'s daughters, played by Nicole Eggert and Susan McClung, would also make an occasional appearance. In 1983, Stacy graduated to street patrol with veteran cop Jim Corrigan (former teen idol James Darren) as her partner.

Heather joked that her part on *Hooker* was so minimal that it didn't allow her to show off her freshly honed acting talents. "Now that I've finally learned to act, there's not much real acting for me to do," she complained at the time. "On *T. J. Hooker*,

"I don't have a money tree growing in my backyard," she told an assistant director one day. "I like to work."

I act helpless and get pulled out of a lot of jams by male cops. It's not exactly Shakespeare. The lines I've had like, 'The license to the red car is . . .' are kind of hard to bring to life."

Her greatest challenge, aside from transforming Stacy's pixy ponytail into a sizzling Sammy Jo-ish coif as the limo took her back and forth between tapings, was remembering all those vowel-ending names. "It's hard keeping all the bad guys straight," said the twenty-year-old actress. "There are so many of them and their names change from week to week. There's a Manicotti in once script and then there's a Minnelli in another. It gets confusing."

And while *Dynasty* was the jewel in the crown of her career, *People* magazine voted *Hooker* one of "The 10 Worst Shows for Women" in 1984. "I think it's chauvinistic, but that's probably because William Shatner's on it," she told a reporter, adding that she sometimes felt intimidated by the famous TV thespian.

"When it's your show, you can't be wrong. You wouldn't see Captain Kirk—I mean T. J. Hooker—doing something wrong. It kind of frustrates me, because I'm always wrong. He's supposed to be a hero, and heroes can't do anything wrong. Right? I always had at least one line, but I was so nervous I couldn't always get it out. I would get really nervous when Bill Shatner would talk to me."

Opposite: "It's not exactly Shakespeare."

Shatner's *Trek* partner Leonard (Spock) Nimoy appeared on *T. J. Hooker* as a cop sent off the deep end by the rape of his daughter. Other celebrity cameo players included Jerry Lee Lewis and the Beach Boys.

Heather also had some "artistic" differences with the show's producers, who complained about the way her police uniform hid her curves. "No one has an upper half in them," she huffed. "And I really looked like a boy; so they gave me these big old padded boobs and underwear with butt pads."

After a few uncomfortable weeks, Heather told the producers to take their padded briefs and stuff it. "It was awful," she said. "And the funny thing was, no one could even see the busty look because I was behind the desk all the time. I told them,

Heather told the producers to take their padded briefs and stuff it.

'There's no way I'm wearing those, and you can take the padded bra with you, too!'"

Not that Heather had any illusions about why she was hired. "We didn't expect that we were getting Bette Davis in the latter stages of her career," quipped Rick Husky, *Hooker's* supervising producer.

Even today, Shatner speaks reverently about Heather's main attractions. "Her skin, eyes, teeth, all exude health," he said. "She's the criterion by which the clean, sexy, athletic California blonde is measured. The ultimate pinup."

As a result, sometimes Heather had to fight to keep her

WHO'S WHO IN THE CAST OF
T. J. HOOKER
MARCH 13, 1982, TO SEPTEMBER 17, 1987

SGT. T. J. HOOKER:
William Shatner

OFFICER VINCE ROMANO (1982–85):
Adrian Zmed

OFFICER STACY SHERIDAN:
Heather Locklear

CAPT. DENNIS SHERIDAN (1982–85):
Richard Herd

FRAN HOOKER (1982–83):
Lee Bryant

VICKI TAYLER (1982):
April Clough

OFFICER JIM CORRIGAN (1983-1986):
James Darren

Hooker was voted one of "the 10 Worst Shows for Women" by *People* magazine

43

The *T. J. Hooker* producers tried to show Heather both in uniform and out of it.

clothes on. Like the time producers asked her to do a dramatic scene in a bikini. She flatly refused. In another episode Stacy was given an undercover assignment as a go-go girl. Heather took it all in stride.

"Sure, some of those scenes are strictly to show off what's under the uniform," she conceded at the time. "I'm not wild about that. But it comes with the territory. Ultimately, if I didn't like playing these characters I wouldn't do it."

Heather prevailed once again on an episode called "Nightmare." In it, Stacy, who suffers amnesia after a car accident, becomes the victim of a psychotic doctor. Heather insisted on doing many of the scenes without makeup and figure-revealing clothes. When it was over, her performance was widely praised.

"Heather never had any sense that she was beautiful," Shatner said recently. "She had no sense of her appeal. I think she knows she's desired by America now, though."

Not Yet a Movie Star

One might think it would have been enough for an actor to have two TV series running at the same time. Not for Heather. "I don't have a money tree growing in my backyard," she told an assistant director one day. "I like to work."

And her hard-work ethic was beginning to pay off. In 1983, only three years after leaving college to become a full-time actress, Heather won Hollywood's Golden Apple Award as Discovery of the Year. When she walked up to the stage to accept her award, her throat went dry and her eyes filled with tears. Memories of the timid girl from high school came flooding back. She was scared speechless.

"I knew in advance that I was getting the award," she recalled. "But when I went up on stage just to say thank you, I began crying and couldn't say a word."

Heather's career was on a roll, and she took on even more projects when *Dynasty* and *Hooker* went on hiatus. In 1984, she did a TV movie called *City Killer,* starring Gerald McRaney (*Major Dad*) as the cop, and Terence Knox as a deranged suitor who terrorizes a city by blowing up skyscrapers in order to impress love-interest Heather. "[It] simply doesn't have the bang," wrote critic Leonard Maltin, "although the demolitions are real."

Ironically, Heather would later become the real-life victim of a deranged stalker. She first became aware that something was wrong when she returned home one day to find her beloved Maltese toy spaniel missing from the dog run. She immediately called the police, who set out in search of the pet. Tragically, the

dog's body was found several hours later by a friend on a near-by hillside.

According to police reports, the dog had been shot twice with a .22 caliber weapon in the backyard and then dumped about one hundred yards behind her property. "There were no witnesses and no evidence of any kind that would link anyone to the shooting," said Lt. Tim Goffa, who investigated the incident for the Animal Regulation Department. Although the killer was never found, fortunately for Heather and her other pets, he never returned.

Heather continued to squeeze in other TV movies between stints on *Dynasty* and *Hooker,* including the highly forgettable *Body Language, Highway Casanova,* and *Her Wicked Ways.* In 1988, she costarred with Dyan Cannon in a slightly better Disney production called *Rock 'n' Roll Mom.* Heather played a bratty teenage rocker renamed Darsey X, who becomes an overnight hit as a pop music star. She auditioned for the part in her boyfriend's studded leather jacket.

With all these small-screen notches on her belt, she longed to break into feature films. But all the scripts that came her way were lousy. It wasn't until she came across the screenplay for *Firestarter,* an adaptation of a Stephen King novel, that she decided to seriously pursue the part.

"I saw a copy of the script and I knew I wanted to play the part of the mother of the little girl with telepathic powers," she said. "They didn't come to me—I went to them. I auditioned for it and got it."

At age 23, Heather played the mother of nine-year-old Drew Barrymore (*ET*), whose character had the ability to shoot real daggers of fire from her eyes. "It's not exactly typecasting," Heather said of her role at the time. "For one scene they had me standing behind a kitchen counter making a meatloaf, telling Drew, 'No!' It felt strange, as if I were doing a cooking commercial or something. I hope no one notices she's almost as tall as I am—and probably more mature."

In truth, the movie's 1984 debut went largely unnoticed by just about everyone. *Firestarter* fizzled miserably at the box office. One reviewer called it "the worst film ever made from a Stephen King novel." Since *Firestarter* had a chilling effect on her film career, Heather fell back into the safer and more welcoming arms of TV.

Opposite: Heather in the TV movie Dirty Work with Linda Purl.

Boys, Boys, Boys

While Heather was still in college, she was engaged briefly to an unnamed beau, but broke it off by mutual agreement. "I would have been a married little girl," she explained. She said her girlish appearance made it difficult for men to approach her. "I was athletic and not overly concerned with my looks," Heather recalled. "As I picture myself, I had a very youthful face. I think men were embarrassed to come on to me because I had that child side."

As she entered the rarefied circles of the Hollywood elite, her startling beauty made her one of the most sought-after women in Tinseltown. The now famous Heather dated a bevy of boy

> *"The sea is*
> *full of them."*

babes such as Tom Cruise, Mark Harmon, Scott Baio, Chris Atkins, and Andrew Stevens (Kate Jackson's ex-husband).

Her romance with Tom Cruise, one of the biggest movie stars today, began while they were both fledgling actors doing a screen test for a failed TV series. "I was really bad, and Tom wasn't as good as me," Heather recalled. She has steadfastly refused to kiss-and-tell about her relationship with Tom, which by most

Heather on Tom Cruise: "It isn't ladylike to discuss an old boyfriend."

accounts was not terribly serious, saying only that "it isn't lady-like to discuss an ex-boyfriend."

What the boyishly handsome actor clearly did for Heather was introduce her to the world of films. One of their most memorable times together was the night he escorted her to the 1982 premiere of *Taps,* a new experience for the starstruck television actress. "It was my first premiere and I found it so exciting," she gushed. "I felt like a little kid. I couldn't stop star-ing at all the celebrities."

But it was soon apparent that Tom and twenty-one-year-old Heather were moving in separate circles; Heather continued to play in the wide field of potential beaus. "I consider myself a one-man woman, but I'll go out with more than one—I'm doing that now," she confessed to a reporter at the time. "I'm pretty

Heather came close to marrying Scott Baio, best known for his work as Chachi on *Happy Days*.

fatalistic about relationships. Some you win, some you lose. Whatever is meant to be, happens."

How does she know if she's in love? "When you can stay up late, you can get up early—you can do anything as long as you can spend time with that person. And you're not tired."

She described her perfect mate this way: "He should be sensitive, have a sense of humor, and know how to make me laugh. I'm attracted to strong men, but not when they're overly conceited. Physical looks are not the most important factor, but the right chemistry has got to be there."

She said she has always believed in being open and honest with the men in her life, even if that meant being the one to pull the plug on the relationship. "You have to tell the person your true feelings—that you're interested in going out with other guys, or you're not interested in him anymore, or you used to love him but not anymore. You tell him everything."

Opposite: Heather and Scott Baio

Heather's boyfriends also included *The Blue Lagoon*'s Christopher Atkins.

During these early dating years, she would sometimes be attracted to a man other than the one she was seeing at the time. "But the attraction is fleeting," she explained, "unless you want to put your relationship on the line. And while I don't put relationships on the line, I always keep in mind that there are twenty more like him, whoever he is. The sea is full of them."

Her favorite trolling technique: "You give them that eye contact and let them feel there's a little way in." Aside from the eligible pool of bachelors she found in the entertainment industry, she also enjoyed playing coed sports with noncelebs.

"I enjoy the competition and companionship," Heather said of her extracurricular activities. "Actually, I'm not very competitive with women. I'm much more competitive with men. I don't know why."

Her competitive spirit stemmed, in part, from her close relationship with her brother Mark, whom she roomed with as a child and later as a student in college. For several years, Heather shared her four-bedroom home in Tarzana with Mark and a friend whom she had dated briefly in high school, David Blatt.

Heather assured gossip-hungry reporters that her relationship with David was strictly platonic: "I live in my end of the house; he lives in his," she told the press.

And after Mark left for U.C. Irvine, David stayed behind. Heather said she felt safer having someone, especially a man, around the house. "A lot of girls I know have men roommates," she argued. "It's been going on at colleges for years. David is a friend and confidant to me, if and when I need a confidant. He doesn't affect my rapport with other men."

In fact, David was still living with Heather when she first met actor Scott Baio. Scott, who is best known for his role as Chachi on *Happy Days,* became one of Heather's most serious boyfriends. Their relationship, which lasted two years, nearly evolved into marriage.

In the beginning, the couple tried to keep a low profile. So

"I think men were embarrassed to come on to me because I had that child side."

"I live in my end of the house, he lives in his."

when Heather appeared on the 1982 *Battle of the Network Stars,* she was mortified when the host asked, "So what's going on with you and Scott?" The characteristically mum Heather (when it comes to her love life) said, "I don't know. Something's going on—but I won't tell."

A year later, Heather and Scott went public at the widely publicized premiere of the Broadway show *Dreamgirls,* where they appeared with such glitterati as Michael Jackson, Rod Stewart, and the then hot singer Olivia Newton-John. Not since she was seen on the arm of Tom Cruise, was Heather part of such a major Hollywood twosome.

Like Heather, Scott came from a tightly knit, conservative family. The couple would frequently visit each other on the sets of their respective shows. And Heather was present for the emotional last taping of *Happy Days*, when the show celebrated the end of eleven successful seasons.

But the relationship had its stormy moments, and there were rumors of Scott's wandering eye. Still, Heather was deeply in love with him, and he was the first boyfriend to succeed in breaking through her strongly held reserve. Although she wouldn't reveal the cause of her outburst, she was willing to describe the first time she was able to truly express her anger.

"I was on my balcony and I threw a wineglass," Heather said

Andrew Stevens, Kate Jackson's ex, dated Heather as well.

of the incident twelve years before. "And I was so shocked that I did it. For me to throw something [gasps], it's like, 'You, young lady, are out of control!' I like to be very much in control. But I was proud of myself for doing it."

For a while, Heather was madly in love. They discussed marriage, since living together was out of the question due to Scott's strict Catholic upbringing. But Scott's father, who was also his manager, was completely against the marriage. He felt

"I'm pretty fatalistic about relationships."

it would damage his son's image as a heartthrob, especially after *Happy Days* went off the air.

Without Mr. Baio's blessing, and with Heather's star rising as fast as Scott's was falling, the two decided to call it quits. "She's a very nice girl," Scott said in a recent TV interview. "Sometimes [women] have problems that you just can't live with." He admitted that his reputation as a womanizer had spoiled many of his past relationships. "I'm so far from perfect," he admitted, "I'm the biggest pain in the ass you could ever be with."

But Scott has dated more than his fair share of TV beauties since his relationship with Heather ended. His list of past loves includes Nicole Eggert, Pamela Anderson from *Baywatch*, and Nicollette Sheridan. "I was going to marry her," he said of Sheridan. "It just totally fell apart. She broke up with me. She told me this wasn't working out and I said, 'Okay, goodbye.'"

After breaking up with Scott, Heather fell into the arms of another TV sex symbol, her former UCLA classmate Mark Harmon. The two all-American knockouts seemed to be a match made in Hollywood. Mark was also a big hit with Heather's father and, for a while, Heather and Mark were inseparable.

"Mark kinda scared me because he was so overbearing," Heather said of their short-lived romance. "He wanted to keep me just the way I was. He would tell me that he loved me, but it was too intense. Nevertheless, he was always a gentleman. When he started saying things about me, it really hurt my feelings."

Apparently, Mark did not take well to being dumped by his gorgeous female counterpart. He later told reporters that their time together was like an "emotional cup of coffee."

But once again, Heather rebounded quickly. A few months later, she met a guy who was different from anyone she had ever been with before. His name was Tommy Lee.

Heather and Mark Harmon had a short, intense romance.

Beauty Meets Beastie Boy

Tongues wagged madly when word got out that the wholesomely beautiful Heather had fallen for Tommy Lee, the ubiquitously tattooed drummer for the heavy metal band Mötley Crüe.

The two met backstage at a 1985 REO Speedwagon concert. For Lee, a self-styled "rock pig," it was love at first sight. "The first time I saw Heather, I got so flipped out I think I lost part of my mind," Tommy recalled. "When I walked into the party, there was the most beautiful woman I'd ever seen. And she was squeezed into the tightest, shortest rubber miniskirt I'd ever laid eyes on."

He was so nervous about meeting Heather that he sent a friend over to ask for an introduction. "I was so shy," Tommy said. "I couldn't possibly have gone up to her myself."

The reticent rocker eventually summoned the courage to speak. "Hi," he said, kissing her hand. "Nice to touch you." The line seemed to work. The twenty-three-year-old Heather was charmed by his outlaw looks and surprised by his interest in her. "I remember seeing four guys with lots of makeup on and thinking that they must be gay," said Heather. "I was a little naive there. But I was always attracted to what is termed the 'bad boy.'"

The next day, Tommy called Heather's manager, begging for her phone number. Her manager promised to relay the message, which Heather ignored. "I had called like a million times," Tommy said. "I wanted to send her flowers or invite her to something. . . anything, just to talk to her."

But Tommy would have to wait several months for a return call. When they finally did speak again, they talked for hours.

At first, Tommy Lee thought Heather was Heather Thomas from *The Fall Guy*.

Now it was Heather's turn to be smitten. She liked him, despite the fact that he initially mistook her for another TV actress.

"After we hung up, I got a phone call back. It's Tommy, and he says, 'Turn on the TV—you're on right now!' I hadn't been doing *Dynasty* much, and it was Wednesday night, and I immediately knew he thought I was Heather Thomas from *The Fall Guy.* Then I said, 'Maybe you don't want to go out with me, because I'm not her.'"

Apparently, it wasn't the first time Heather had been mistaken for the other blond TV actress with the same first name. "She and I did *Battle of the Network Stars* together, and people kept mistaking us for one another," she explained. "I'm baffled by it. There are a million blondes with a million blue eyes who don't look anything like me. I don't see why I'm confused with her."

But Heather forgave Tommy's blunder, and they met again three days later. He picked her up at her house in Tarzana. Heather took one look at the scruffy man waiting for her to get ready and had second thoughts about her own squeaky-clean image. "I came downstairs, saw Tommy, and ran right back upstairs to make my hair wilder," Heather recalled.

For their first date the couple went to dinner at a romantic Italian restaurant in Los Angeles; afterward they took in the late show at the Comedy Store. Lee, who enjoyed bringing out the wild side in Heather, was head over black boots in love. Heather, who also had a great time, agreed to see him again.

"I know there's a part of me that needs excitement, so I don't sit back and observe, but instead take part in having fun and loosening up," Heather admitted. "I've gone out with really nice men and the excitement wasn't there."

Tommy immediately called his mother to tell her about their date. Heather and Tommy were officially an item. After six months, Tommy wanted to show Heather how deeply he felt for her. He called her from Bloomington, Indiana, where the band was on tour, and held the receiver next to his left forearm. She could hear the hum of the tattoo needle as it etched a big black rose with her name across a banner onto the canvas of his flesh. "I hadn't seen her in a long time," the besotted Tommy explained.

Although Tommy's torso was already covered with tattoos,

Opposite: Tommy Lee: "The first time I saw Heather, I got so flipped out I think I lost part of my mind."

Why would a nice, conservative girl like Heather go for a head banger with a bad rap?

the black rose was, of course, her favorite. "It's very pretty," commented Heather at the time. "Actually, all of his tattoos are pretty, taken one by one."

Heather would eventually get a tattoo of her own (a red rose and heart on her ankle), but it was a decision she would later regret. "It's a mistake over a mistake," Heather said recently. "I'm not gonna say what it started out as, but I didn't like it, so I added to it."

Heather was so afraid of her parents' reaction, that she wore socks whenever she was with them. When her dad finally noticed the tattoo, he looked at his youngest daughter with dismay: "Just don't change," he pleaded.

Not only was Heather changing, but she felt as though she were straddling two separate worlds. TV glam girl by day; rock 'n' roll party girl by night. Tommy made no attempts to hide his rancor for the phoniness that can spread like a virus in Hollywood. He told her one day while they were jogging, "You know, Heather, if my fans see me with a tan and running with you, my career is over."

Still, Heather enjoyed the occasional celebrity function, especially if there was a good cause attached. In 1985, her two worlds merged when Tommy met her *Dynasty* costars for the first time at a glittery AIDS benefit.

"I don't think Joan Collins and John Forsythe could quite believe who had turned up with Heather," Tommy laughed. "We arrived in a limo, and when we stepped out into the theater, everyone was taken aback. Here was a very glamorous Heather Locklear with some wild-haired rock star in a tuxedo." Much to Heather's surprise (and relief), Tommy and John Forsythe ended up drinking bourbon together at the bar later that night.

Dynasty producer Aaron Spelling recalls his first impression: "I remember when she brought Tommy over and said, 'I want you to meet my fiancé.' I almost had a heart attack. She was my little girl. How dare she do that? And how dare he do that?"

To the outside world, they seemed like the ultimate odd couple. Why would a nice, conservative girl like Heather go for a head banger with a bad rap? "There must be something creative about them that I like," Heather said of her rocker fetish. "Maybe I wish I could sing—I don't know. . . . I tend to think I'm so exciting that they're drawn to me."

After all, it was Heather who once said that the swashbuckling actor Errol Flynn was the man she most admired because he represented danger and nastiness. Through Tommy (the modern Flynn), Heather was making a statement about her straitlaced upbringing. "Looking back, it must have been some form of rebellion," she recently concluded. "You do what I can't do, so I'll watch."

But despite his bad-boy image, Heather insisted that the real Tommy was "wonderfully sweet" and had a terrific sense of humor.

"I think she likes that little edge, because she isn't that way," Heather's mom surmised. "She is just so straight and a little shy herself."

Tommy, on the other hand, was at a loss to explain their mutual attraction. "Don't even ask me why we're so well matched," he once said incredulously. "I have trouble sometimes dealing with it myself. Here is Heather, a top Hollywood star. . . . She's a sex symbol for millions of guys; and then there's me, just a wild rock 'n' roller. And she loves me! It's crazy."

Of course, Heather and Tommy did have a few things in common. Both were Californians; both were extremely close to their families; and both had gained wealth and success at an early age.

Born in Greece, Tommy and his sister Athena were brought to the United States in 1965, when their father, David, took a job as a shop superintendent for the Los Angeles County road department. His mother, Boula, was a housewife who had won the Miss Athens title in 1957.

As a teenage rebel, Tommy was expelled from South Hills High School for skipping every class except gym and shop.

Tommy eventually graduated from Royal Oak High, where he had learned to play the drums by joining the marching band. At seventeen, he made the rounds of L.A.'s rock clubs before hooking up with a band that became Mötley Crüe. The band's first album, entitled *Too Fast For Love,* sold 800,000 copies and established them as one of the top-selling and longest running heavy-metal groups today.

he Engagement

On Christmas eve 1985, Tommy proposed to Heather while riding in a limousine back to her house. He stuck his head through the sunroof and asked Heather to join him. With their long hair flapping in the wind, Tommy reached into his pocket and placed a 2.3-carat diamond ring on Heather's finger.

"Will you marry me?" Tommy shouted. "Yes!" Heather yelled back. "Now get back down here!"

In honor of their engagement, Heather used some money she had earned on TV to buy Tommy a $32,000 customized guitar that was once owned by Jimi Hendrix. It is a gift that he treasures to this day.

Tommy's parents were thrilled to hear the news of their son's impending nuptials. His first marriage, to model Elaine Bergen, had ended after only seven months. This one, Boula Lee was convinced, would last. "They're perfect for each other," she told a reporter. She advised Tommy to love and respect Heather and to "treat her like a lady"—not like "one of those groupies."

Heather's dad was not as eager to accept the hard rocker into the family fold. He had adored Mark Harmon and was disappointed when his daughter's relationship with the actor had ended. "I got this stomachache," Heather recalled about breaking the news of the engagement to her dad. 'You're getting married?' my father said. I couldn't even answer, I just nodded. 'To Mark?' he asked. I swear to God that's what he said. I was so nervous."

Tommy remembered the day he was first introduced to Heather's father. Bill Locklear had called Heather unexpectedly to say that he was coming over to the house for a visit. Tommy, who was sunning himself by the pool, immediately jumped into action.

"I'm pulling earrings out and putting on a long-sleeve shirt," Tommy recalled. "And when he comes in I'm sitting like a gentleman by the pool. I think her dad thought I was crazy sitting there in ninety-degree heat dressed like it was freezing."

But Tommy's cover-up did little to impress Mr. Locklear. "Who does he belong to?" the disapproving dad asked Heather and her sister Colleen, who was also staying at the house.

In time Heather's parents learned to overlook Tommy's rough-edged image. "Tommy's just a real up and warm person," Heather's mom once remarked. Diane and Bill gave the young couple their blessing.

"He had earrings and long hair, but they weren't against us getting married at all," Heather said.

Of course, Heather's girlfriends threw her a bridal shower, complete with lacy lingerie and sex toys. And Tommy's boisterous stag party was exactly what one would expect for a rock star on the precipice of marriage; the guests were entertained by fifteen beautiful, bikini-clad mud wrestlers.

The Wedding

On May 10, 1986, approximately one year after their engagement, Heather and Tommy exchanged vows before five hundred guests at a lavish ceremony in Santa Barbara's Biltmore hotel. The wedding was held in a palm-shaded courtyard festooned with gardenias and tulips. The place and time of the nuptials were kept under tight wraps, and thirty security guards were enlisted to keep the press and gate-crashers at bay.

As the string quartet began the wedding march for Heather's walk down the aisle, Tommy, who wore an eyebrow-raising

"I've only thought of getting married once."

white leather tux, casually tossed his gum in the bushes. Heather was followed by her four bridesmaids—two sisters and two friends, all dressed in black. Nikki Sixx of Mötley Crüe did the honors as best man.

The guests sighed their collective approval when the bride appeared in a strapless, skin-tight mermaid-style dress. The

What a Mötley Crüe!

$2,000 white satin-and-lace gown was adorned with pearls and sequins. A full-length tulle veil, a pearl-studded ivory headpiece, and long white lace gloves completed the breathtaking ensemble.

Heather giggled nervously throughout most of the forty-minute ceremony, which ended with a dozen white doves fluttering above the newlyweds as they sealed their vows with a passionate kiss.

At the reception afterward, guests sipped champagne to the tunes of (who else?) Mötley Crüe. A sky diver leaped from an airplane and descended slowly upon the gathering leaving a pink trail of smoke. "It's so exciting," gushed the radiant bride. "I can't believe it's all happening . . ."

The ever-skeptical media predicted that the union wouldn't last. David Letterman gave the marriage only fifty-six days. But like all newlyweds, Heather was sure that she and Tommy would be together forever. "I've only thought of getting married once," the twenty-four-year-old bride told a reporter. "I plan for this one to last."

The groom was similarly optimistic: "I think we'll be the coolest grandma and grandpa in the world," Tommy said. "We'll be like eighty-five or ninety—I'll still be a rock pig, and Heather will still be gorgeous."

The couple were so certain of their commitment to one another that they refused to sign a prenuptial agreement. "That's only for suckers like Madonna or Joan Collins," Tommy

David Letterman gave the marriage only 56 days.

scoffed. "We know our love is gonna last."

Yet the marriage showed signs of trouble from the beginning. Just two days after the couple was wed, Heather and Tommy reportedly got into a knock-down, drag-out fight during their honeymoon in the Cayman Islands. According to one item in the press, the local police were called in to break up the squabble.

But the newlyweds quickly patched things up, and they returned after three weeks to Heather's lavish Tudor-style home, which now reflected both their lifestyles. For a while, the marriage seemed to be rock solid.

Tommy's gold and platinum albums adorned the walls. The study was converted into a recording studio and gym, with an eight-track system for Tommy and free weights for the fitness-conscious Heather. The living room had a tanning machine so Heather could catch up on her rays, and a drum set so Tommy could catch up on some practicing.

When Heather did not have an early call on the set, the couple would start their day sometime in the afternoon with a large breakfast of scrambled eggs and sausage prepared by Tommy. "He's someone who always needs to be busy," Heather said, "whereas I'm a person who just likes to lie back and cruise."

Heather admitted that Tommy's high-decibel tastes in music, "took a while to get used to." But she was relieved to discover that her husband also craved peace and quiet when he wasn't on the road. "He really doesn't listen to music constantly at the house," she said.

But music was never too far from his thoughts. "Music is always on his mind," she said. "He seems to be preoccupied at times because he's so hyper, and because he's always dreaming and pounding on things. I think musicians are a different breed because they live and breathe their music. When they watch television they listen to the background music. And they're creative. Their whole life is run by music."

For the first year, the couple's frequent separations seemed to make their hearts grow fonder and the marriage stronger. "I personally think it's the best setup in the world," Heather said of Tommy's road trips, "because of my independence and his. I don't like someone around me all the time, and he doesn't either. He's used to being on the road and not being with someone twenty-four hours a day. And when I see him on the weekends, or every other weekend it's the best! We make the most of the time we have!"

Tommy agreed: "We just can't leave each other alone," he said. "We lock the door to the house, turn on the stereo, and just forget about everyone for two or three days while we make up for lost time." (Heather later said that sex with Tommy was so great that she "could see the back of the inside of her head.")

Although Heather eventually wanted children, she knew their hectic careers made it impossible to start a family right away. Besides, neither of them were quite ready to settle into domesticity. For a while, Heather shared Tommy's love of liquor and his fraternity-like passion for partying.

Tommy: "Deep down in her heart, she's a real rock 'n' roller. And she'll drink Jack Daniels like a rock trouper. She loves the stuff. We'll slug our way through a bottle in a night."

"There's nothing cool and sophisticated about [Heather] when it comes to play," Tommy said in a 1986 interview. "Deep down in her heart, she's a real rock 'n' roller. And she'll drink Jack Daniels like a rock trouper. She loves the stuff. We'll slug our way through a bottle in a night.

"I've been used to spending all my time with rock people, drinking and swearing and joking, but Heather can match them all when she gets going. She adores clearing off from the *Dynasty* set and jumping in the car and cruisin' the rock clubs. I call her my little partner-in-crime because we have such a good time together."

Opposite: Many wondered what the girl-next-door saw in the heavy metal rocker.

The Bad Old Days

The good times wouldn't last forever. Tommy and his band went on a number of well-publicized hell-raising rampages. During one concert at Milwaukee's Bradley Center, Mötley Crüe's lead singer, Vince Neil, was almost arrested for inciting a riot when fans trashed the stadium and clashed with police.

In 1984, Neil had spent thirty days in jail for smashing into an oncoming car while driving drunk. His passenger died tragically in the accident, and Neil paid $2.6 million in restitution to the injured couple in the other car.

After that, the entire band stopped driving, but they did not stop drinking and drugging. By this time Tommy was an admitted alcoholic who also used cocaine and heroin. It took Neil's near-fatal heroin overdose to get Tommy and the rest of the Crüe into rehab.

"One night I just stared at a beer in the minibar," Tommy recalled. "I thought, 'Tommy, you can't fall off the wagon for one measly beer. Order up a bottle of Jack Daniel's. Do it right.' But then I got a grip and got the hell out of there." To help the band stay straight, a drug counselor was enlisted to regularly meet with them on tour.

Although Heather often joined in the revelry, drinking appeared to be her only vice. Her closest brush with the law occurred in 1988, when she and Tommy were questioned by police after stepping off a plane in Jamaica. Also detained was their traveling companion, Leigh Bruce Ritch, the partner of prominent record promoter and Mötley Crüe manager Doc

McGhee. Although Heather and Tommy were never charged with a crime, Ritch was arrested and later sentenced to thirty years in prison on pot- and cocaine-smuggling charges.

Of course, the band whose credo is "being all things to all men and a lot more to all women" was constantly pursued by groupies (and pursuing them). Although Heather denies it, it has been said that Tommy's infidelities caused the marriage to disintegrate. "Tommy was an alcoholic who went through bimbo after bimbo," said a friend of Heather's.

Tommy himself alluded to his wild lifestyle as a rock star on the road. "I work for an hour and forty minutes a day," he said, "I have another twenty-two hours to play. I shouldn't really say that much, but you can probably imagine some of the things that are going on."

In addition to the omnipresent female fans, there were

"Monogamy is extremely important."

reports of Tommy's uncontrollable anger. "He was abusive. . . ," said a friend of Heather's. "Heather once told me about the violence—her scuffles with Tommy and the bruises he gave her."

Another Hollywood insider also knew of the violent fights that occurred during the seven-year marriage. "One time Tommy was furious with Heather for not doing something he'd asked her to do," the source revealed. "He yelled and screamed at her until she was in tears. Then he grabbed her by the shoulders, shoved her against the side of their house, stuck his face right in hers, and screamed some more. Heather was hysterical. She looked like she'd been through this scene before—and she didn't want it to go any further. Finally, she fled in tears."

But Heather was not ready to call it quits. She tried her best to cope with the rumors of her husband's indiscretions, dismissing them as simply tabloid fodder.

"Hey, honey, I heard you were arrested for showing your thang," she laughed.

"Monogamy is extremely important," she insisted publicly. "It has to be. And no exceptions. The woman can always do the same thing, and I'm sure no man would like that."

Heather threw herself into her TV career, deciding to believe Tommy's assurances that he had never strayed. "You have to be secure in yourself," she told the reporters who dogged her with stories of the band's carousing.

"If you don't have that, you're going to cause a lot of problems in the marriage by pointing the finger—'You did this, or don't do this'—or whatever. As for me, I want my freedom. I'm giving him his. You know, 'Do what you want, I trust you.' What those guys do on the road when I'm not around is all fine and dandy. I'm not worried."

For Tommy, whose band produced such records as *Girls, Girls, Girls,* those were words to live by. "Now don't say that kind of stuff unless you mean it," he told her afterward. "I don't want to be heartbroken."

Heather tried hard to maintain her laissez-faire attitude toward Tommy and the band. After hearing about his arrest in 1990 for indecent exposure, Heather phoned Tommy that night at his hotel in Cincinnati to tease him. "Hey, honey, I heard you were arrested for showing your *thang,*" she laughed.

"Naw, gorgeous," Tommy said. "I just hung a BA." Tommy had apparently mooned someone in the audience.

And to help keep her husband in tow, she would fly to wherever he was playing on the weekends. But as the years passed,

Heather's patience with Tommy's on-the-road antics wore thin. "I worry about him," she later admitted to a reporter. "I'd be lying if I said I didn't."

The fights began to get louder and more frequent. During one argument, the normally reserved Heather lost her cool. "One time I threw this basket of fruit on the table and yelled at my husband, 'Well, what about me?!' I think I actually surprised him. Because I usually never lose control."

By 1992, just a year before their split, Heather and Tommy saw a counselor in a last-ditch attempt to save their rocky marriage. "I go [to a therapist] once a week," Tommy said at the time. "I go with my wife, and it's great. I'm still learning how to have a relationship. It's like a referee to us."

Heather had also persuaded Tommy to join Alcoholics Anonymous. She asked him to go with her for an AIDS test after hearing that Althea Flynt, the wife of *Hustler* magazine publisher Larry Flynt, had died of the disease. Tommy had once shared a needle with Althea.

"My wife and I were talking about getting tested," Tommy said at the time. "Who knows? I used to share needles with some psychos. So, man, I think about it all the time. God forbid it's true."

The Final Straw

Despite efforts to solve their marital problems, stories of Tommy's debauchery continued. The tabloids reported that Heather once walked in on Tommy having sex with a model in his hotel room. "She's put up with his wild ways almost from the time they married," said a friend of Heather's. "But even she has her limits."

Tommy called the story "bullshit," while Heather refused to comment on the rumor. "Honestly, though," Heather said. "Tommy was bummed that he wasn't matched up in the story with someone better-looking."

To make matters worse, Tommy started having his own bouts of jealousy. It drove him crazy whenever his wife was called upon to do a love scene with her handsome costars. "People are always giving my husband a hard time about it, 'Ooh, your wife is always kissing everyone,'" Heather said, only months before she separated from her husband. "I think that may bother him. It would bother me."

The final blow, according to several reports, came the day she heard that Tommy had shared a hot tub with a gaggle of groupies. "The straw that broke the camel's back, from what I heard, was when he was bragging backstage about being with some babes in a hot tub," said Los Angeles magazine columnist Ed Dwyer. "Word got back to her, she called him on it, and he admitted to it. She essentially said that she had had it."

That week, in August of 1993, Heather filed for a divorce. She continues to publicly deny that Tommy was ever unfaithful to her. "If that happened," she said, "he did a very good job of covering it. We married too young—at twenty-three and twenty-four. We just kind of grew apart."

"[I was] raised not to talk bad about people."

Unlike many high-profile celebrity divorces, Heather maintains a tight-lipped policy about her marriage to Tommy Lee. "It's like airing your laundry or something," she said. "[I was] raised not to talk bad about people."

Tommy has also refrained from blaming Heather for their divorce. "Heather is an awesome girl," he told Howard Stern during a recent interview. "We just never saw each other, man. She

was doin' her thing and I was doin' mine. I mean, why be married when you never see each other? What's the point? A little space is cool, but months at a time, why be married?"

After the Fall

Tommy's troubles seemed to multiply after the divorce. In February of 1994, he got into his first of several serious jams when he tried to carry a .40-caliber semiautomatic pistol aboard an airplane.

He was arrested when the airport security officer discovered the gun and ten hollow-tip bullets in his carry-on luggage. Tommy pleaded no contest. He was eventually released and placed on a year's probation after paying the $1,000 fine for possession of a concealed firearm.

Six months later, his band, which had enjoyed great success in the past, was forced to cancel their tour because tickets weren't selling fast enough. And on September 22, just two weeks after his divorce from Heather became final, Tommy got into a free-for-all brawl at the House of Blues in Hollywood.

The rumble started around closing time. First, Tommy's friend got shoved around. Then the quick-tempered Tommy got into a scuffle with a security guard twice his size. "He was very belligerent and he was screaming obscenities," said photographer E. L. Woody, who witnessed the melee. "[Tommy] tried to

Tommy Lee's new wife, Pamela Anderson of *Baywatch*.

strike one of the other people there and had to be restrained by the security guards, and later by the police."

Video footage taken that evening shows four cops struggling to control the drunken drummer. "The police came over, grabbed him by the hair, and lifted him up," recalled Woody. "He knocked their hands off and struck the officer so they just grabbed him up, pinned his hands behind his back, and cuffed him. I recognized him when I saw the tiger-striped tattoos on his back." The police managed to restrain Tommy by temporarily blinding him with a blast of pepper spray. No charges were filed.

But Tommy lost control once again that December with his fiancée of-the-moment, twenty-five-year-old rock video model Bobbie Brown. Bobbie reportedly flagged down a police car outside Tommy's home in Malibu, asking the officers to stand guard while she collected her belongings. When a deputy escorted her back into the house, he heard Tommy and Bobbie resume their argument.

"The deputy asked Bobbie to leave, and as she did so, she said that Tommy had beaten her," reported a source. "The deputy detained Tommy and requested a crime unit to come to the house to conduct a criminal investigation for possible physical abuse."

Bobbie told the police that the couple had another row a week earlier when she was late getting ready to go out. "She said Tommy entered the bathroom and began yelling and cursing at her," a source revealed. "When she responded, Tommy grabbed her around the neck with both hands and slammed her back into the bathroom wall. Tommy then lifted her off the floor by her neck." The attack lasted about thirty seconds, until Tommy's sister came in to break it up.

Bobbie was left with bruises on her neck and scratches on her right arm. The police arrested Tommy for misdemeanor spousal abuse before releasing him on $50,000 bail. When asked to comment on the incident, Tommy insisted that he was innocent. "This is all bogus," he said. "It didn't happen anything like she says it did. She hit me first."

Bobbie broke off the engagement. But Tommy would not be single for long. After dating for only one month, Tommy and

Pamela Anderson, a star on the wildly popular *Baywatch* series, eloped to Cancún, Mexico, on February 19, 1995. Witnesses said they tied the knot on a pier, where the bride wore white—a white thong bikini—and the groom wore trunks.

It remains to be seen if this marriage has a fighting chance, since Tommy has gone public about his having a working wife. "I'm not into the career-woman thing anymore," he said in a magazine interview. "I just want my woman by my side. Is that too much to ask?"

Lean, Mean, and Back on the Dating Scene

Following her separation from Tommy, Heather's phone remained strangely silent. "I didn't get a lot of phone calls from guys after people found out I was getting a divorce," she said. But Heather enjoyed her brief cooling-off period, spending most of her free time with her family and friends. "I'm not devastated or destroyed," she said soon after the breakup. "It's mostly just sad."

Nevertheless, she said her divorce from Tommy was one of the most painful experiences of her life. "No matter what, it hurts—it kills. It kills your heart. Because when you get married, you want it to be forever. And some things just don't work out that way."

Never one to dwell on the negative, Heather decided to turn

But her self-imposed celibacy didn't last for long.

the pain into something constructive. "It's good that whatever pain I go through, at least I get to use it. It's not just 'Here's some pain in your life—so sorry.' At least I get to use mine. . . . It's sad, but hopefully you grow stronger."

With the help of a therapist, she was able to put the past behind her, while vowing to learn from the mistakes of her first marriage. "I've learned so much about myself by being married, about being with another person, commitment, what my strengths and weaknesses are, what I'll compromise on and what I won't. . . . I used to say 'whatever you want,' and inside it wasn't what I wanted. I learned to open myself up, but I'm still learning how to do that."

But her self-imposed celibacy didn't last for long. She was later spotted by item-hungry gossips with two of her *Melrose* costars: Andrew Shue and Grant Show (now engaged to Laura "Sydney" Leighton).

Although her relationship with Andrew was mostly platonic, she was seen in a passionate embrace with Grant at a Hollywood flea market in March 1994. A month later, the couple was politely but firmly ejected from the trendy Union Square Cafe in Manhattan for their alcohol-induced boisterousness, according to a "Page Six" item in the *New York Post*. The duo later turned up at another New York City hot spot called Club USA, where they boogied with the late night crowd till 4 A.M.

Heather was having fun again. She enjoyed dating Grant, but there was someone else who had caught her eye: Bon Jovi guitarist Richie Sambora.

Opposite: "I didn't get a lot of phone calls from guys after people found out I was getting a divorce.' "

The Lean Years

In the spring of 1985, *T. J. Hooker* was mercifully canceled. It was picked up briefly by CBS but finally died at the end of the 1985-86 season. Heather dived back into her *Dynasty* role, increasing her on-screen time as Sammy Jo. But in May of 1989, *Dynasty* finally reached the end of its long run. Its spin-off, *The Colbys,* never got off the ground. The heady eighties were nearly over, and Heather was a free agent for the first time in years.

After both series ended, few offers came in to fill the gap.

"I thought, 'Should I have a baby now?'"

Her career had taken a sudden, and serious, nosedive. It was time for Heather to take a personal inventory to decide what her next step should be. Perhaps she should take a hiatus from Hollywood, she thought. She could concentrate on her marriage to Tommy and spend more time with him on tour.

"I thought, 'Should I have a baby, now?'" Heather recalled of her career lull. "What should I do? I was taking accounting classes. I thought I should figure out my money before I lose it."

But Heather was itching to get back to work. So in 1989, she

Heather has a fling with a Swamp Thing.

took her second feature film role in *Return of the Swamp Thing,* based on the DC comic, in the hope that it would resuscitate her career. "I thought it was a horror movie until I read it, and I always wanted to do a comedy."

But *Swamp Thing* failed miserably as both a comedy and a science fiction movie. In it, Heather's character Abigail falls for an algae-covered superhero after learning that her stepfather, played by Louis Jourdan, has similar designs on her. It seemed the evil stepdaddy, a Dr. Arcane, has this ugly habit of blending people with animals.

"Is there a Mrs. Swamp Thing?" Abigail asks the former Dr. Alec Holland coyly. "I'm a plant," the man who gathers moss replies. "I'm a vegetarian," she counters. Later she muses while caressing a fern: "Why can't men be more like plants? You can stroke plants and they don't get the wrong idea."

But Swamp Thing *liked* being stroked by Abigail. In fact, she seemed to rub him the right way. Was it difficult for Heather to feel romantic toward a plant? "It was a little trying," she admitted after the filming. "I had to concentrate on his eyes. I kept thinking there was a man under there."

The reviews were uniformly awful. Leonard Maltin called it "oafish," and the film won Heather a nomination for the Golden Raspberry Award as the worst actress in 1989. *The Washington Post* said *Swamp Thing* was "a catalogue of bad acting unredeemed by humor, and it will quickly settle back into the swamp of anonymity accorded most minor comic book heroes."

Heather bravely bit the bullets of criticism and returned once again to the trenches of television. In the fall of 1989, she costarred in a TV movie called *Jury Duty: The Comedy* with credit-heavy actors such as Alan Thicke (*Growing Pains*), Bronson Pinchot (*Perfect Strangers*), Lynn Redgrave (*Chicken Soup*), Danny Pintauro (*Who's the Boss*), William G. Schilling (*Head of the Class*), Barbara Bosson (*Hooperman*), and Tracy Scoggins (*Dynasty/Colbys*).

Jury Duty was about a group of jurors whose lives are turned upside down when an extortion trial turns into a sensational media circus. The *New York Post* called Heather's performance as a hooker-juror "strangely subdued." And with the exception

Opposite: All-woman meets all-vegetable.

of Pinchot, who played four different parts in the movie, the reviewer said Heather and others in the cast "neither get nor add very much."

But Heather found the experience pleasurable. "I'm used to working with an ensemble," she told a reporter . "One of the reasons I took this job is that it's really fun to be with a different group of people and a new crew."

In September 1990, she premiered with Alan Ruck, Jerry Levin, Hallie Todd, and Holland Taylor in a sitcom about TV comedy writers called *Going Places.* It involved a team of four neophytes thrown together to write gags for a *Candid Camera*-type series called *Here's Looking at You.*

Heather played Alexandra "Alex" Burton, a sexy but naive woman from Denver. She and her fellow writers all lived together and played pranks on one another in a Los Angeles beach house. The conflict came in the form of the tyrannical and neurotic producer Dawn.

When audiences stayed away, the show was completely revamped. The series within a series was canceled and the foursome became a production team for an egotistical talk-show host named Dick Roberts and his frenetic producer Arnie. Despite efforts to salvage it, *Going Places* went nowhere, and it, too, was canceled, in July 1991.

Heather also made a TV movie for ABC called *Rich Men,*

Swamp Thing failed miserably both as a comedy and a science fiction movie.

Going Places with, top row, Alan Ruck, Holland Taylor and Hallie Todd. Bottom row: Heather and Jerry Levine.

Single Women with Suzanne Somers and Deborah Adair. The movie, which premiered on January 29, 1990, was a takeoff on the fifties hit film *How to Marry a Millionaire* with Marilyn Monroe, Betty Grable, and Lauren Bacall. The TV version was about three zany singles who hatch a plan to entrap some loaded guys. They move into a ritzy Malibu house (on the beach again!) that Suzanne Somers is supposed to be selling as a real estate agent.

People magazine gave *Rich Men* a D–, remarking that, "this sexist idiocy is really a cleaned-up version of those bimbos-in-a-beach-house movies that gurgle to the surface on late-night cable without ever seeing a theater." And the normally forgiving populist paper *USA Today* said, *"Rich Men, Single Women* is an entertainment so light that it must have floated in from some parallel universe where romantic comedy is evil torture. Adair does the best here, clinging to a modicum of dignity throughout. Locklear is button cute. Somers should take a crack at an exercise video." (This was pre-Thighmaster, of course.)

Heather even ventured onto the stage, taking a role in *I Hate Hamlet* at Florida's Jupiter Theater. When that ended, she used some of the money she had earned on *Dynasty* and *Hooker* to form her own production company called Lockit Productions. She hoped that it would help to get good scripts sent her way. It didn't.

Fitness Video

Nothing seemed to be clicking for Heather, which didn't stop her from branching out even further into other media. In 1990, she made a modestly successful exercise video called "Your Personal Workout."

The hour-long tape, which is still available at many rental stores, features a pixie-haired Heather leading an energetic group of buffed-up dudes and dudettes in an aerobics class. Wearing a pink thong and blue tights, Heather, who never appears to break a sweat, shouts "How's everybody doin'?" and "You guys are awesome!" as she leads the class through a routine of pelvic thrusts and stomach crunches.

With the exercise era in full swing, Heather was also hired as a spokeswoman for Bally's national chain of fitness clubs. She was once again doing TV ads, for which she received some Amanda-like flack from Bally's former celebrity promoter.

"I wrote the last commercials—all of them—myself," Cher sniffed in a 1988 *Playboy* interview. "So now it pisses me off that Heather Locklear is doing them! (*voice rising*) I produced the commercials, wrote the commercials . . . it was *my* concept and I feel invaded because I didn't write that commercial from my life to have some blond bimbo of twenty-five stick her tongue out at the end of it!"

Heather ignored the rebuff. She was down, but she was never totally out of the picture. Her love of performing and belief that she would someday bounce back to the top of her profession kept her spirits high all through the rough patches.

Opposite: Cher was none too pleased to be replaced by Heather as Bally's spokes-bod.

Heather's exercise video.

Heather was not the only one to star in her own exercise video. Here's how the list shapes up so far. (An asterisk indicates the Fox-y ones who have appeared on *Melrose)*.

Dixie Carter
Cher
Joan Collins
Cathy Lee Crosby
Cindy Crawford
Sandy Duncan
Britt Ekland
Morgan Fairchild
Jane Fonda

Jennie Garth*
Mary Hart
Marilu Henner
Shirley Jones
Angela Lansbury
Traci Lords*
Joan Lundon
Marla Maples
Rita Moreno
Stefanie Powers
Debbie Reynolds
Jaclyn Smith
Suzanne Somers
Lindsay Wagner
Jody Watley
Raquel Welch

eather's Career Resurrection

Of course Heather's star would rise once again, thanks to *Melrose Place* and a fledgling network called Fox-TV. Creator Darren Star said he developed the concept for the series directly from his own life.

"I had an idea for a show about people in their twenties living in a courtyard apartment building in L.A.," he said. "I had been through that experience myself—I lived in an courtyard apartment building with a pool in the L.A.–Hollywood area, which certainly didn't look like the one on *Melrose Place,* but it was the same idea."

Although he never lived on or near Melrose Place, Star decided it would make a great backdrop for a show. "I think Melrose Avenue represents what's sort of hip and fun and young about L.A.," he said. "It's where young people come to start their careers, find themselves, and define themselves. Melrose strikes me as the center of all this. . . . They were excited about it at Fox, and we just went from there."

The Fox executives may have liked the idea, but the American public wasn't so sure. Initially the series languished like a cold latke. The group of sweet but ambitious twentysomethings struggling to make their rent was not enough. The only danger in the storyline was the possibility of falling asleep.

That's when mega-producer Aaron Spelling, whose three decades of hits include *Mod Squad, Starsky and Hutch, Charlie's Angels, The Love Boat, Dynasty,* and *Beverly Hills*

**Heather's Amanda gave *Melrose Place* the injection
of the soapy sizzle that it needed.**

90210, came galloping in on his white cellular phone. He called Heather to ask if she would do him a favor.

"What we had in the beginning was a very interesting, but very passive, group," said Spelling. "We had this devoted doctor who kept apologizing for not making love to his wife because he was too tired, for instance. . . . We needed Heather to stir up the pot." He asked her if she would agree to guest star on just four episodes.

Although her own career was in a slump, Heather did not jump at the chance to do another TV series. She was still eager to make her mark in feature films. So she consulted her manager, who advised her that her appearance on a failing show would not be a career-buster. "It's probably not going to help you and it's not gonna hurt you," her manager told her. "So do whatever you want."

Heather consented, figuring she had nothing to lose. "If the show did well because I was a guest star, I could say it was all me—yuk, yuk, yuk," she explained. "But if it got canceled, I could say, *'Please*—this show was on the way out.'"

As it happened, Amanda Woodward gave the show the injection of soapy sizzle that it needed. "They wanted to add a character who could lend conflict and put some fire under the other characters," Heather said. "It was a bunch of nice people talking nice about each other, which is very nice, but who cares? . . . Before Amanda came, the characters on the show were just trying to get jobs and saying, 'Poor me.' Amanda gave

Heather did not jump at the chance to do another TV series.

them something to fight against."

They also transformed Michael from an overworked intern into a self-serving, womanizing scoundrel. In the second season, they added the emotionally disabled Sydney to wreak even more havoc. The complex was getting more complex and the ratings skyrocketed practically overnight. The show finally had a much-needed, back-stabbing, boyfriend-stealing villainess at its center.

"There's an old Noël Coward expression that fits: 'to put the cat amongst the pigeons,'" said Spelling. "We needed Heather to be the cat amongst the pigeons."

For playing the cat woman of Melrose, Heather is reportedly receiving $40,000 per episode, up the from $15,000 she got for

Remember the Molly's Cookie campaign? You know, the one that Amanda dreamed up as a way to outrage a client and mortify Alison? It went something like this: a businesswoman gets a craving for something sweet. She sees a truck filled with Molly's Cookies parked outside her office window and dives head-first into the van. The tag line: "There's never a bad time to dive into Molly's Cookies." Unfortunately for Alison, the client's mother had committed suicide by jumping off a building. But hey, who knew, except maybe Amanda?

Here's what Carol Demelio Corbett, senior vice president and associate creative director at Wells, Rich and Greene in New York had to say about the pitch:

I like the idea of someone in a totally different situation, because you usually see kids and cookies, not executives, because children probably eat more cookies than adults. So Amanda's idea could be visually and strategically interesting. But the ending is pathetic. To use that kind of tag line is weak. In real life, though, a disastrous campaign like this one could have been avoided by having a team of people discussing the idea before presenting it to the client.

doing the first four guest shots (it could be more by the time this book is published). With thirty-two episodes per season, that means the current Queen of TV is now making well over a million per year. And if ratings equal revenue, it is money well spent.

"She single-handedly saved *Melrose Place*," declared *Los Angeles* magazine's Ed Dwyer. "The numbers don't lie. The show was in a tailspin until she got there."

TV columnist Matt Rousch of *USA Today* had this explanation for Heather's head-spinning turnaround: "I think it's the fact that when she left *Dynasty*, that genre of the prime-time soap

Aaron Spelling: "Heather should be playing a nun."

that had flourished in the past was beginning to fade. But when the Fox Network came along and created *Melrose Place* it was time for her to come back. She could never have been the lead character in *Dynasty*. But she can now be the diva of a new generation. *Melrose* without her probably wouldn't be on the air anymore."

Of course, there were a few naysayers among the critics, such as Matthew Gilbert from the *Boston Globe*. While crediting Heather with salvaging the show, he added: "*Melrose* has saved her as well, from an eternity of movies of the week. Her delivery is delightfully mediocre—she's an emotionally disabled Farrah Fawcett."

*In honor of the show, a new restaurant opened in Hollywood called Melrose Place.

*Grant Show and Doug Savant also dropped out of UCLA.

*There's a real street called Melrose Place. It's off Melrose Avenue, home of the young and trendy.

*Shooters is a real bar on Melrose Avenue called Trinity.

*The actual address of Amanda's digs is 4616 Melrose Place. But don't try to find it—the show is filmed in Santa Clarita.

*The original Billy Campbell was replaced by Andrew Shue.

And *Time* magazine's Richard Zoglin was equally unimpressed: "Heather Locklear, whose addition to the cast . . . as the bitchy Amanda is credited with turning the show around, doesn't have the evil-doing pizzazz of a Joan Collins or Larry Hagman."

Try telling that to the viewers, the ultimate judges, who watched in droves. The success of *Melrose Place* has been so overwhelming that the actors themselves are at a loss to explain it. "There used to be a lot of nighttime soaps, but there haven't been so many lately," observed Andrew Shue. "So I think it fills that void."

Grant Show had his own theory: "It's not a soap—it's serious drama" he joked. "I think the show's a little different because it's so campy."

With this overnight swell of popularity, it would have been easy for Heather to throw all of her hundred-odd pounds around as the show's acknowledged savior. But there have been no rumors of behind-the-scenes bickering à la Delta Burke or matriarchal takeovers à la Roseanne. And good luck trying to find someone on the show to say a bad word about her. In fact, stories of Heather's unwavering good humor and cooperativeness abound.

Heather's easygoing attitude was particularly apparent the

day she was given the wrong directions to a location by someone on the production staff. As a result, Heather found herself hopelessly (and conspicuously) lost on the mean streets of South Central Los Angeles.

When she finally phoned in to the studio for help, she was surprisingly composed. "No problem, don't worry about it," she told the astonished crew "I'll just be a little late."

And Heather remained similarly unperturbed when her dyed dress started to bleed—turning her milky white skin a revolting shade of pink. While the wardrobe director went ballistic, Heather laughed it off as she searched for something else to wear.

"It was a bunch of nice people talking nice about each other, which is very nice, but who cares?"

Grant Show: "It's not a soap—it's serious drama!"

"She was incredibly gracious and calm," said the grateful dresser. "And she did the whole scene after that with her skin bright pink."

Because Heather did not enter *Melrose Place* brandishing her ego like an unsheathed sword, her fellow actors harbor no resentment toward her heroic status. "You would think everybody on the set would loathe Heather," Spelling said incredulously. "She gets all the covers, all the publicity—but they adore her. I can't figure out what makes her tick. Heather should be playing a nun."

Even her on-screen nemesis is an admirer. "She deserves a lot of credit for our success," said Courtney Thorne-Smith (Alison). "She brought an element we really needed—the villain—and her energy. It's a better show now."

Of course, Heather was grateful for the warm reception she received from the cast. "Who knows how anyone might have reacted if we'd known in advance how things were going to turn out? But as it was, I was just another guest star coming in, and everyone was really friendly. The actors here know this is a job."

And despite the laudatory response to her arrival on *Melrose,* she has refused to take all of the credit for the show's success. "The writing changed," she said modestly. "It really didn't have a lot to do with me. I think I brought a certain number of people to view it, obviously the ratings jumped, but beyond that you have to keep somebody's interest. I was on a sitcom before for a year and no one tuned in. So thank God I've got some fans out there who wanted to see me, and they got hooked."

Amanda the Hun

What makes the character of Amanda Woodward so universally loved *and* reviled? That has been the subject of much speculation by pop-culture pundits and insiders alike. *Melrose* creator Darren Star believes Amanda is like a workingwoman's Joan of Arc—a warrior on a male-dominated battleground and a product of women's hard-won advances in the business world.

"When women began assuming more powerful positions in society, they could become villains on television on parity with men," he suggested. "I think people look to Amanda as a role model. She's going out there, fulfilling her own agenda, and creating her own sense of power. And I think that's empowering to a lot of women."

Heather agreed: "Women want to see women have the upper hand," she said. "Fully. Across the board. No equal fairness here. We've seen how an assertive woman is called a bitch.

"I'm an important advertising executive, you bastard."

Well, maybe. In a chronicle of fashion failures, *Glamour* magazine chided Amanda's working-woman wardrobe for being too sexy for the boardroom. "What has worked for Amanda is the little tiny suit with the short skirt and tapered waist," defended *Melrose* costume designer Denise Wingate, creator of the Amanda look.

Yet her signature body-hugging jackets and miniskirts leave some female executives cold. "Amanda stretches the idea of dressing for success," sniffed Roberta Meyers, senior editor of *In Style* magazine. "It's more like dressing for excess."

Other real-life female execs say workingwomen should avoid emulating Amanda's wardrobe. "Amanda is absolutely projecting the wrong image," insisted Ellen Dominus, ad sales planner for the MTV Network in New York. "How can she sit in a meeting without looking like Sharon Stone in *Basic Instinct?* She should definitely wear pantyhose. . ."

Apparently, even L.A.'s more relaxed offices are not ready for the bare-legged look. "If Amanda wants to wear the pants at the agency, she should wear some pants *to* the agency," said Sharon Hall, V.P. of programming at BBDO in Los Angeles. "But even in L.A., going barelegged is downright unprofessional."

Glass ceilings aside, Heather is happy to have Amanda get a few wolf whistles while she works. She has asked Denise in wardrobe to take the hems up even higher. And that's okay with viewers, according to the folks at *Melrose,* who have been swamped with letters asking where they can buy her sexy bizduds. The producers have responded by coming out with a new line of "Amanda" clothes.

In the meantime, anyone interested in buying the sexy, thigh-high power suits that Amanda dons each week, can find them at Bebe (pronounced BEE-bee). The bicoastal women's clothing chain has been selling lots of *Melrose*-inspired fashions to hip, young business types.

Heather on Amanda. "I'm going to sleep with as many men as I can, and then I'm going to cross over to women, too. It's probably an issue we should explore."

How men have the power and get taken seriously when women don't. Women want control. Is that a reality? No. But if you want to watch reality, watch a movie of the week."

If Amanda is not quite what Gloria Steinem had envisioned as the love child of the feminist movement, she is by far one of TV's most enjoyable bad-girls. As a pal, she can't be trusted with your boyfriend; as a boss, she can't be trusted with the intercom; as an employee, she can't be trusted with your clients; and as a businesswoman, she is someone whom sharks avoid out of professional courtesy.

The fun began as soon as Amanda landed her job as supervisor at D&D Advertising. She immediately made a play for Alison's boyfriend, Billy, causing a rift between the roommates turned lovers. And if that wasn't torture enough, the well- and

Amanda (Heather) with her mother, Hilary Michaels (Linda Grey) on *Models, Inc.*
the ill-fated *Melrose* spin-off.

"I watch Melrose Place for sex, sleaze, horrible writing, and nothing else!" commented one regular in the Melrose chat group on America Online.

high-heeled Amanda purchased the apartment complex where Alison and Billy resided, guaranteeing her place as ruler of both roosts.

Yet Amanda is as much of an outsider as she is leader of the pack. Having left her twenties behind her, she is not a member of Generation X. But in the battle of bods and brains, she is clearly the victor.

"When you watch Heather Locklear play Amanda Woodward, you have the same delicious certainty that you're going to get exactly what you want just as you do when you order a cheeseburger, large fries, and a chocolate shake at McDonald's," observed Nancy Franklin, theater critic for the *New Yorker*. "She never disappoints. Amanda is the smartest character by far, and though she's ruthless and selfish—and, horror of horrors, a *landlord* as well as an advertising maven—she's the most

sympathetic character on the show.

"She knows who she is, she knows what she wants, and she's fearless about going after it, but she's not a monster. She's a cartoon, and an oddly touching one, because Locklear is very competent in keeping Amanda from going over the top; she plays her at or near the top—taking risks, making herself vulnerable to the dimwits surrounding her—so that when she falls she falls hard, and believably."

Marshall Blonsky, who deconstructed the show for *Spy* magazine, also had kudos for Amanda: "[Amanda] is the only one with some intelligence and plenty of sexiness," he observed. "Amanda is allowed to do things that the others are not allowed to do. She is allowed a permanent scowl. She is also allowed to own Melrose Place. Amanda is not among the constrained, but at a price: she's also not afforded the general group empathy."

It's a shame, too, because Amanda could do with some poolside tea and sympathy. An undisputed winner in the heartless world of business, she is undeniably a loser at love. She trolls her homey little harem like a blond bottom feeder, scavenging for Alison and Jo's sloppy seconds. She slept with Billy, got pregnant, miscarried, and lost him to Alison. She stole Jake from Jo, only to have him snatched away from her by a murderous boat bimbo. Even her malevolent male counterpart, Dr. Burns, dumped her for his ex-girlfriend, Caitlin.

"Yeah, she likes leftovers," Heather said of Amanda. "I'm going to sleep with as many men as I can, and then I'm going to cross over to women, too. It's probably an issue we should explore."

Of course, Amanda's voracious appetite for sex and power can be traced back to her highly dysfunctional family. "Amanda was abandoned by her mother when she was just eleven," Heather explains. "She latched on to her father, who taught her to be ambitious. Obviously, we don't want to see the bad things in those we love. Learning the truth about him puts her into more confusion about who she is."

And when asked to explain Amanda's emotional range of A to B, Heather said: "Amanda almost has the core of a man. She thinks and acts like one to a certain extent. Maybe that's because her father raised her. In most of her scenes, she doesn't want to talk or reveal her feelings."

Opposite: Amanda (Heather) with Billy Campbell (Andrew Shue). Why is Amanda always waking up alone?

"I watch it because it's fun," explained über-model Cindy Crawford, who interviewed the *Melrose* cast for one of her TV specials. "It's, like, an escape."

And if, like, critical raves and ratings can be believed, *Melrose* has done for Cindy's generation what Woodstock did for her parents'. Some see it as an opportunity to get together with their pals each week to discuss the bad acting, continuity errors (sharp watchers will see objects mysteriously appear and disappear after jump cuts), or the latest contortionistic plot twists.

"Hey, if I want normal relationships, I'll watch *thirtysomething* on Lifetime," commented one regular in the *Melrose* chat group on America Online. "I watch *Melrose Place* for sex, sleaze, horrible writing, and nothing else!"

The show's over-the-top plot lines and character portrayals are enjoyed by cultural elitists as well.

"[*Melrose Place*] is the kind of show you fall for in spite of yourself," wrote Elizabeth Kolbert of the *New York Times,* "the way you sometimes buy clothes you wouldn't actually be seen wearing in public.

"I often watch it with friends, many of them educated at name-brand institutions and some of them, by E. D. Hirsch's standards at least, even culturally literate. No one talks during the show, and it is considered bad form to object to an episode on the basis of something trivial like, say, plausibility."

Why has *Melrose* captured such a demographically diverse audience? Perhaps it's because *Melrose* is a soap opera about people we can fantasize being most like ourselves. Unlike its posh progenitor *Beverly Hills 90210,* Melrosers actually work for a living. Amanda pulls a double shift as ad exec and landlady; Billy and Alison are wage slaves; and Jake is a bar owner.

And where the *Hills'* gang are, for the most part, wholesome, Melrosers can be bad to the bone. The show's creators have mercifully replaced the dreary morality plays with good old-fashioned murder, lust, and ambition. In other words, it's our deepest fears and fantasies come to life with all the subtlety of a Punch and Judy show.

A Los Angeles Times TV critic had another explanation for the phenomenon: *"Melrose Place's* feature players are all as pretty as models and dumb as oxen—allowing us to feel covetous and superior all at once, a pretty addictive mix."

Clifford Winston, senior fellow at the Brookings Institution, had his own reasons for watching: "The sex, intrigue—that's not what I care about," he sniffed. "What I like about the show is it's California oriented. Living in the East and being an academic, I'm around nerdy people who are hypercritical of efforts at sustained excellence. To me, Southern California is gorgeous people who are totally supportive of superficial efforts at mediocrity. I watch and think, 'God, wouldn't it be nice to have a constituency like that?' "

Psychotherapist Will Miller, Ph.D., who makes an occasional appearance as Nick at Nite's Freudian spokesman, has analyzed the current *MP* obsession: "Seeing our mistakes played out (sometimes to melodramatic extremes) may serve the therapeutic purpose of propelling us into action." Hmmmm.

If playing the emotionally repressed and sexually charged Amanda comes naturally to Heather, playing the bossy Amanda does not. "Amanda takes charge of business, which I don't want to," she said. "It's very uncomfortable for me to play those scenes where Amanda takes charge of a meeting. The other side of her is so easy for me. Doing it on a desk—easy."

But it was a role that Heather was ready to play in her real life as well. "When I met Aaron [about the series], the next step in my career was playing an assertive, strong businesswoman rather than a girl," she recalled. "I was going through a period in my life where I needed to be assertive and strong. Maybe the program was a safe place for me to experience those feelings."

And in a condo full of twenty-somethings, Heather enjoys playing the Melrose matriarch. "I love being portrayed as the older-woman-as-cradle-robber for a change," she said. "And I didn't want to play a twenty-year-old anymore. If I did it, I would feel like I was cheating the audience—and cheating myself. I've done that for thirteen years."

During the first few seasons, Heather worked closely with the writers to develop Amanda into a bitch goddess with brains. "It had nothing to do with the age; it was about wanting to be mature. I said she has to be an ambitious career woman who is intelligent. And they said, 'Okay, okay.' So for four episodes they did that—and then in the fifth episode, they made me bad!"

At first, Heather thought they might have gone too far, so she asked them to make Amanda a bit more sympathetic. "It's fun being bitchy," she said, "but when it started becoming apparent that Amanda has this bad side to her, it was written in such a black-and-white way. [So] I tried as much as I could to play against that. If I didn't, it would just be like somebody twirling their mustache. We had discussions about needing to show a little vulnerability in Amanda and other things they were writing. And now it kinda works."

Then, Heather began to wonder why the more vulnerable Amanda was always waking up alone? "I asked the writers, 'Is there any way that some guy would just *like* Amanda and stay with her?' They just said, 'Yeah, yeah, yeah.' And I'm thinking, "What's wrong with that chick—why can't she get someone on her own? Amanda is lonely. But we never see her as that. I think it would be really nice to see those subtleties."

Later she switched gears once again, afraid that Amanda's character had become "too nice." At this point, the exasperated scribes threw up their hands and said, "Well, what the fuck do you want?" But the bitchy Amanda had already caught on with the viewers, and Heather quickly slipped back into her role as the show's villainess.

Today, if Heather does any lobbying at all, it's for an unkinder and less gentle Amanda. When Amanda was charged with sexu-

Michael Mancini to Amanda: "You and I both know that you can get a Tibetan monk to strip naked and dance the hoochie-koochie if you wanted to bad enough. Or if there were something in it for you."

al harassment by her mother's two-timing lover, Heather said she secretly wished for more than "the group hug at the end."

She thinks Amanda should unleash what might be her hidden, kinkier fantasies. "I would have Amanda do really offbeat stuff, like go to a humiliation-sex club," Heather suggests. "Get some tattoos! Rough her up a bit. Something different, weird. I don't know if Amanda would don the gear, but she could watch. We would see her reaction, her darker side. I'd like to see her say, 'I have to finish this meeting, so I can get to the club!' She carries the whip in her briefcase. And a black mask. Just a little hardcore."

For now, Amanda must be content with verbally chastising her underlings like a dominatrix with a laptop, or luring them into her executive lair for a roll on the desk. Simply stated, there are no limits to what she would do to advance her career.

"She never *deliberately* sets out to hurt anyone," said Heather, in defense of Amanda's survival instincts. "If she has to save her ass, she'll do it. Just like we all do."

And Heather isn't the least concerned about the reality-impaired viewers who shout at her to "Leave Billy alone!" while she is walking down the street. "If they don't like me, they don't like me." She shrugged. "I'm doing my job correctly. Big deal. I'll go into another part where I will be liked, if that's a big concern of mine." It isn't.

What does the National Association of Female Executives have to say about Amanda Woodward's management style from hell? "She sabotages people; she asks underlings to join in conspiracies against other employees; she sleeps with people on the job; and she's betrayed her own mentor," said NAFE director Wendy Reid Crisp, who watches the show each week with her son's twenty-year-old girlfriend. "She's taken every single woman executive buzzword for the last twenty years and driven a nail through it."

The fact that Amanda is a walking Not To Do list for professional women does not bother Crisp. "A little part of all of us aspires to be Amanda, but we can never be that calculat-ingly vicious," she said. "If we were, we'd be punished forever for it because women are not allowed to be that self-absorbed. A lot of us would like to be able to handle our political problems in business in the way Amanda handles hers.

"After you've answered a hundred phone calls from people whom you don't necessarily like, and then you've taken phone calls from friends and family who need you for one reason or another, it's nice to spend an hour watching someone who does exactly what suits her on any given moment. It's a fabulous fantasy Who wants to watch someone run a great meeting, or call people in one-by-one to tell them what a good job they're doing?"

Richie Sambora: I do, I do

Heather was introduced to Richie Sambora by her best friend and makeup artist Lisa Christy shortly before her divorce from Tommy. According to one source, the thirty-five-year-old musician was instrumental in getting Heather to leave the two-timing Tommy.

"Richie sat down backstage at the Roxy Theater in Hollywood," a pal of Heather's said. "He told her, 'Tommy is out of control. Booze and groupies are part of his lifestyle—and he's

"I like everything about him."

never going to change. It's time to get on with your life.' "

A tear rolled down Heather's cheek as she listened to Richie's advice. "I know," she said sadly.

Heather left Tommy soon afterward, and Richie continued to stay in touch with her by phone. They started dating in February, 1994. "We definitely didn't have dinner," Heather said enigmatically of their first date, "but we didn't have anything we weren't supposed to have either."

Their relationship had been rumored for months before Heather spilled the beans to Howard Stern during a telephone interview from her hotel suite. The raunchy radio host kept pressing her about whether she was seeing Richie, until she finally said, "Here, ask him yourself," before handing the phone to her bedmate.

"Can you believe this?" the bemused Richie said.

"If this isn't the best advertisement for guitar lessons," quipped the victorious Stern.

Although their relationship developed at breakneck speed, Heather wasn't always so taken with the baby-faced guitarist. According to one Hollywood source, Heather once remarked, "Richie Sambora has the ugliest mouth I've ever seen! He's really one big nothing. And why is he dating Cher?"

Of course, as anyone who has ever read a tabloid knows, Richie and Cher were one the hottest celebrity couples between 1989 and 1991. "I helped her straighten out a lot of stuff in her life," Richie said, "and she helped me straighten out stuff in mine. Cher was one woman who took care of me. I don't mean she would make me sandwiches and wash my clothes. I mean in an emotional way. When she would talk, I understood her. When I would say something, she understood me, deep."

Richie first met Cher while he was cowriting "We All Sleep Alone" with Desmond Child for her 1987 album. They started dating seriously when their paths crossed again two years later.

Although Richie wasn't ready for marriage, it was Cher who told him that the relationship wasn't working out. "Basically, she told me to take a hike," Richie said. "Not a hike—that's the wrong term—but she was feeling very pressured because she had a tour, a movie, and a record and also family stuff to deal with. And I was doing my thing and was all over the place."

By the time Richie met Heather, his attitude toward marriage had changed dramatically. He first popped the question in July of 1994. But whenever the subject of marriage arose, Heather refused to discuss it. Not enough time had passed since her separation from Tommy. She needed to learn how to trust again.

Opposite: Heather with Richie Sambora

A tear rolled down Heather's cheek as she listened to Richie's advice. "I know," she said sadly.

But Richie persisted, asking, "Do you think you're ready?" every few weeks.

On September 10, 1994, just weeks after her divorce from Tommy became final, Richie presented Heather with a huge pear-shaped Cartier diamond set in platinum.

The next day the couple appeared for the first time in public at the Emmy awards. They must have had quite a celebration that night, because an exhausted-looking Heather could barely keep her eyes open during the ceremony.

"Heather looked like she was going to nod off at any moment," observed a fellow guest. "She yawned through the whole show."

And when the duo was stopped by reporters backstage, a clearly besotted Richie remarked, "I don't understand why *she's* not nominated," while Heather smiled nervously beside him.

"Richie's very happy, ecstatically happy, with Heather," said a friend of the band. "With all of the women he's been with— Cher, Ally Sheedy, Becca Bramlett, those *Playboy* women— none of them have lit a candle for him next to this one."

Richie met Rebecca Bramlett, daughter of sixties songwriters Delaney and Bonnie, at a Moody Blues concert where she was performing as a backup singer. "We talked until the wee hours of the next morning," recalled Rebecca, now twenty-seven. "The next day he sent me flowers in my hotel. The card said, 'To a true lady from a true gentleman,' and I went, 'I do have to go out with the man!'"

But another former love of Richie's said that Heather might be hitching herself to disaster by marrying the rock star. Lehua Reid described Richie as a domineering, womanizing booze-hound. "I don't know if Richie was ever faithful to me," whined the thirty-two-year-old aspiring model and actress.

Around Christmas 1987, Lehua pulled up stakes in L.A. and moved into Richie's New Jersey home. She would remain there for the next two years. "The first year we were going out, we were pretty inseparable," she recalled. "But during the second year it was a different story, and I don't have any doubt that he probably had several affairs that year."

Although Lehua described Richie as a wonderful lover, "the sex was great," she said his passion soon faded. "Richie has had some of the most beautiful women in the world, and he's either cheated on them or dumped them when he got fed up."

After a while, Lehua added, Richie began to show his darker side. "He never beat me physically, but emotionally it became a nightmare," she said, "and the battles always began when he'd been drinking too much. During the day he would drink wine coolers and then go on to vodka and rum. He drank too much, and so did I when I was with him. I once begged him to stop boozing for a week when my thirteen-year-old niece came to visit. He couldn't do it."

According to Lehua, Richie would forbid the curvaceous model from showing too much skin in public. "He didn't like

Richie and Cher were one of the hottest celebrity couples between 1989 and 1991.

"With all of the women he's been with—Cher, Ally Sheedy, Becca Bramlett, those Playboy women—none of them have lit a candle for him next to this one."

me dressing in anything revealing or sexy," she said. "When we were at the American Music Awards in 1988, we ended up in a huge fight. He told me I looked like a tramp and said, 'Did you see David Lee Roth staring at your breasts?'"

Lehua predicted trouble for Heather down the road. "I was surprised to see the clothes that [Heather] wears," she said, "because when I was dating him, I would never have been allowed to wear anything like that. I see her in these sheer outfits with cleavage and I think that someday he's going to complain."

To make matters worse, Lehua claimed that Richie would continually question her fidelity, even though *he* was the one doing the cheating. "He was always accusing me of hitting on his friends," she recalled. "It got to the point that I was cowering like a dog while he was yelling and screaming at me. He screamed so loud that he spit in my face."

Richie, who has never hidden his past problems with alcohol, eventually sent Lehua packing. Lehua said he had her clothes shipped C.O.D. to her grandmother's house in Los Angeles. Soon afterward, he began dating actress Ally Sheedy.

"It didn't really last long—a couple of months," Richie said of his tumultuous relationship with the former brat packer "I was going through a bout with alcohol at the time. And she was going through a drug period that I had no idea about. I was on tour, and she was breaking up with me all the time.

"I dealt with this for a few weeks and finally I just went, 'Fine, then fuck it.' I didn't take any calls anymore. I was kooky myself, and I split for Hawaii. The next thing I knew, she was in a rehab center. I tried to call, but the doctors didn't think it was a good idea for me to talk to her."

Despite the fact that Richie's history of booze and babes was not unlike her ex-husband Tommy's, Heather has assured her worried friends that she was not about to have her heart broken twice. She swore that he was "nothing like Tommy" and that he knew "if he did mess around, and I found out, I wouldn't wait to strangle him when he came home—I'd be gone."

So Heather and Richie made a pact. In exchange for his promise to be faithful, Heather agreed to tone down her TV love scenes. "Heather talked to Aaron Spelling about her engagement," said one insider. "She asked him if she could cut back on her love scenes because they drove Richie crazy."

"Here's a little secret: I've never been pregnant in my life."

"I've always wanted to marry my father."

Heather also asked Richie to cut all ties with his ex-love Cher. "Richie kept up a phone relationship with Cher, and Heather never liked it," a friend of Heather's revealed. "She thinks it's unhealthy to keep in such close contact—no matter how platonic it may seem."

And there have been signs that Heather has helped Richie put reckless days behind him. Orange juice has replaced alcohol as his beverage of choice, and he is even careful to wear a seat belt while driving. "I've changed my ways," he said. "I'm totally in love with Heather. She's a great girl."

There have also been numerous reports about Heather and Richie's desperate desire to have a baby, which she adamantly denies. Asked if she was, in fact, eager to a have child, she shrugged and said, "Not particularly. When I was twenty I was really ready to have a kid, and now I'm really not. I like my life the way it is: time with my husband and work."

About those other rumors that she is already pregnant. "Here's a little secret: I've never been pregnant in my life."

The couple are so deep in the throes of passion that Heather often beeps Richie when she is between taping scenes for *Melrose.* They have been frequently seen stealing away to Heather's dressing room trailer. But there are other reasons why Heather feels she and Richie are a perfect match.

"Richie is more like my father," she said of her second husband. "He's very gentle, very kind, loving, and mature—and very supportive. I've always wanted to marry my father."

A self-described "eternal optimist," Richie hails from Woodbridge, New Jersey, where he has stayed close to his fam-

MEN WANT TO CHARGE IT WITH HEATHER

According to a 1994 survey sponsored by the Factory Outlet Marketing Association, 19 percent of the men polled said Heather was the woman they would most like to go clothes shopping with. She beat out the scantily dressed siren Sharon Stone, who received 16 percent of the men's vote.

Only 6 percent of the women selected Heather as their favorite shopping companion—a dead heat with First Lady Hillary Rodham Clinton.

Heather's favorite purchases: clothes, furniture, sheets, shoes, and beige lipstick.

ily. "He told me about the house he had bought for his parents," recalled Lisa Bernhard, who profiled Richie for *US* magazine.

"He was about two hours late for the interview because he had been on a radio station playing requests from the seventies. I was starting to get pissed off, but the second he walked in the door I couldn't be mad—he was so warm, friendly, and nice."

In fact, he and the other band members, born west of Manhattan, are cut from the same cloth that produced working-class hero Bruce Springsteen. The last to sign on with Jon Bon Jovi, Richie went backstage after hearing the band for the first time and said, "We should be working together."

At the time, his musical c.v. included being a guitarist for the little-known metal band Mercy; a member of Duke Williams and the Extremes, a funk band on the Allman Brothers' label; a vice president of his own label; and a try-out for Kiss.

"I rubbed Jon the wrong way instantly," Richie recalled. "He just kind of went, 'Ha, ha. Who is this asshole?' " But after only one rehearsal, Richie became Bon Jovi's second in command.

Softer than the head-banging Mötley Crüe, Bon Jovi continues to have a devoted mainstream following, and the band is closer to Heather's own musical tastes. "We're safe," explained Richie. "We're not heavy metal, but we're certainly not pussy rock, either."

The Weddings

On December 15, 1994, Heather and Richie quietly exchanged vows before Judge Milberg and a small group of family and friends in Rumson, New Jersey, where Richie keeps a home.

"I built and lived in the house that I later sold to Richie, so he thought it appropriate that I be the one to marry them," said Judge Milberg. "I was honored to be part of such a special moment."

The next day the couple flew off to Paris, where they did it all over again on December 17 at the American Cathedral. "I wanted to get married in Paris because it's the most romantic city in the world," Heather told a friend.

But the couple had to be married first in the states in order to make the union legal. "I'm not even going to kiss you," she told Richie before the deluxe ceremony on the continent, "I'm saving myself." True to her word, the bride and groom stayed in separate rooms and arrived in separate limos until "the real wedding," as Heather called it, was over.

To her Paris wedding, the bride wore an off-white gown with a French lace halter bodice over nude silk chiffon, a matching bolero jacket, and a heavy Swiss satin skirt. The gown was the work of *Dynasty* designer Nolan Miller, who had whipped up the dress just four days earlier.

Apparently Heather had decided at the last minute that she did not like her original choice, and she called the Los Angeles

Married life seems to agree with Heather.

designer for help. The elegant ensemble reportedly cost between $10,000 and $17,000. Last-minute adornment was a necklace of pear-shaped diamonds that matched her engagement ring, a surprise gift from Richie.

At twelve thirty on Saturday afternoon, Heather stepped out of her limo holding a can of hair spray that she had grabbed as she was leaving the hotel. "She got so nervous, she almost carried it with her down the aisle," said one witness. "An attendant took it from her as the music started."

Many of the guests, which included both sets of parents and Bon Jovi bandmember Tico Torres, had received their invitations in a holiday gift basket along with a bottle of champagne and a

All told, the extravagant nuptials were estimated to cost a whopping $350,000

round-trip ticket to Paris. The couple, and their two dozen or so guests, all stayed in $500-a-night suites at the exclusive St. James's Club, where Heather and Richie registered under aliases to avoid the press.

How did Heather's parents feel about their daughter's mar-

According to a survey of personal trainers, Heather is said to possess one of the "most influential female bodies," along with super-athlete Jackie Joyner-Kersee, mega-model Elle MacPherson, and the terminally buff actress Linda Hamilton.

Heather, however, is quick to find fault with her own seemingly perfect physique. "I'm knock-kneed," she complained. "[My knees] can look at each other and have a conversation. I have to walk on the edges of my feet so my knees can be a little straighter."

Because of this, Heather has asked the *Melrose* wardrobers to hike up her hemline. "My legs look too thin if you don't see a little muscle, which is up higher," she explained.

riage to yet another rocker? "We love Richie," Diane Locklear said. "He and Heather are so much alike. His goals are the same. He's very close to his mom and dad, just like Heather."

"Heather didn't plan on this," her mom continued. "You don't plan on falling in love or finding the right person, but if you don't take it while it's here, you could lose it and never find it again."

After the heavily guarded, forty-five-minute ceremony was over, the celebrants drove to the Ritz hotel, where they toasted with champagne and $100-a-glass Remy Martin cognac from the Louis XIII period. The reception, which lasted well into the night, included a sit-down dinner of scampi, veal tenderloin, sea bass, and rice. For dessert, the guests had a choice of either French cream custard or tiramisú.

"Heather wanted it to be the perfect wedding," said a friend. "She's been planning this since she got engaged to Richie in September." And Heather spared no expense this time around. All told, the extravagant nuptials were estimated to have cost a whopping $350,000.

The Honeymoon

After taking in the sights of Paris, the newlyweds jetted off to Hawaii in Bon Jovi's private Boeing 707 for the second leg of their honeymoon. The plane, which the band uses for its concert tours, has a master bedroom, several wet bars, and a hot tub.

Waiting for them at the oceanfront mansion owned by millionaire hairstylist Paul Mitchell was a trunk filled with warm-weather clothes and sexy new lingerie from Victoria's Secret. According to reports the newlyweds did not emerge from their Oahu compound for the next thirty-six hours.

A friend and neighbor, who visited Heather and Richie at the estate, said there were dozens of presents underneath a beautifully decorated Christmas tree. One of the wedding gifts was a $10,000 diamond tennis bracelet from Heather's doting Fox executives. Their other present to Heather was too large to fit under the tree: a brand-new $90,000 white Mercedes-Benz.

When the couple finally ventured out, they headed for the elegant Assagios restaurant, where they feasted on a $400 meal of seafood and champagne. "I guess Richie must have been hungry, because he ordered tons of food—clams, shrimp, oysters on the half shell, and several bottles of our best Dom Perignon," their waitress Sandra recalled.

In addition to romantic strolls on the beach and frolics in the surf, the couple toured the islands by helicopter, shopped at the Aloha Tower boutiques, chartered a catamaran to explore an outer reef, and danced at a trendy south side disco.

"Richie and Heather were hugging and kissing in the limo and talking about the helicopter tour they'd taken on Christmas

"Now that I'm married, no more just-the-girls," she sighed. "Now it's just the guy."

Day looking at properties in Maui," said limo driver Bart Bascone, who chauffeured them to the airport.

Before leaving Hawaii, the couple stopped at a phone booth to call a local radio station to thank everyone for showing them a wonderful time. "I almost fell off my seat when I realized it wasn't some nut, said KQNG deejay Ed Kanoi. "It really was the Bon Jovi guitarist."

And Heather was still "completely glowing" from the honeymoon, according to one witness, when she passed out white roses to everyone on the American Airlines flight back to Los Angeles.

Although Heather obviously believes that this marriage will be the one that lasts forever, the couple have signed a prenuptial agreement—just in case. The newlyweds are planning to divide their time between New Jersey and Los Angeles, where they have purchased land in the exclusive Holmby Hills. Although Heather enjoys traveling—"except for the packing"—she said she gets homesick for the Left Coast after about three weeks.

They escape the spotlight by visiting their rustic but cozy cabin at Lake Arrowhead—the place where Heather spent many happy summers as a child and played Pictionary with her girlfriends before Richie was in the picture. It is now the place where glamorous couple likes to chill out, rent a video, and eat in. "Now that I'm married, no more just-the-girls," she sighed. "Now it's just the guy."

The cabin has a loft, three small bedrooms on the ground floor, and large glass doors, which give the living room a panoramic view of the woods. "It's great," Richie told Heather the first time she brought him to the cabin. "It's happenin'. I love what you've done with it. It's like the outdoors, indoors."

What she did was furnish the entire cabin during a single shopping spree at Arte de Mexico in North Hollywood and a raid of her parents' garage. "I just went, 'That! that! that!' and hoped it would fit," she said. One "that" was a $900 chandelier made from naturally shed deer antlers.

"It can be hard for them to get together," observed one friend, "but [their marriage] is something Richie takes very seriously. He's worked hard at the relationship, and he's very, very happy." Though he's no shuscher like Heather, he's agreed to give skiing a try. And one activity they both share is sitting in front of the big-screen TV to watch movies and sports.

Will there be any other changes in attitude this time around? "I'm not going to make the bed anymore," she said firmly. "I'm not going to keep things to myself. If something's wrong, I'm gonna say, 'I don't like that.' And Richie's gonna say, 'Heather, honey, why don't you learn some tact?'"

The Real Heather

As TV's reigning queen of mean, it is easy to imagine that the real Heather is a lot like the character she plays. How else could she be so convincing as the talon-sharp Amanda?

Heather's real dirty little secret is that she's nice.

"Don't ask me about my feelings."

"Haven't you heard of typecasting?" Heather asked ruefully. "I'm a bitch on the show and I'm a bitch in real life."

Don't believe it for a second. Heather's dirty little secret is that she's funny, down-to-earth, and (whisper) nice. No divalike outbursts on the set, and no "I'm ready for my close-up" dementia ."She knows every crew member's name," said *Melrose* assistant director Kevin Duncan. "She always comes in with a smile on her face."

And when Courtney Thorne-Smith first met Heather, she was pleasantly surprised by Heather's intelligence and wit. "I didn't expect her to be so funny, so kind, quick, and self-deprecating," Courtney said. "With the way she looks, why should she develop a personality?"

Daphne Zuniga also took an immediate liking to Heather. "Heather can laugh at herself," Daphne said. "She knows what her image is."

In fact, Heather's ability to parody herself is one of things that sets her apart from the legions of narcissistic Hollywood starlets. Her self-mockery and understanding of her limitations as an actress have disarmed even the most poison-penned journalist.

When asked by writer Michael Musto what her secret for acting in a prime-time soap was for his article in *Vanity Fair,* she said, "Short skirts. It's my skirt that's doing all the acting."

How would she see herself in the role of Lady Macbeth? Musto asked. "I'd be exactly the same," she parried. " 'Out, damned spot—I said out, goddammit!' "

And while Amanda can lash out like a cornered animal at any-

Wanna discuss the latest scratch-your-eyes-out feud between Amanda and (fill in the blank)? Now Heather fans and *Melrose*-maniacs can meet each other on the great info-highway. Just type "alt.tv.melrose-place" into your computer and you will find a bulletin board full of other like-minded viewers.

If you're a member of America Online, you can become a so-called "Placemat," by chatting about that week's show every Tuesday at 10:00 p.m. 'Net surfers can also download an electronic newsletter called the "Melrose Update," which boasts 1,500 subscribers on every continent except Antarctica.

The *Melrose Update* staff examines each and every episode of *Melrose Place* in "excruciating detail," promises Ian Ferrell, the twenty-four-year-old Microsoft manager who started this venture two years ago.

"Respected experts from all walks of life strip the story down to sheet metal and leave no plot complication unexplored. Without shedding a tear, each specialist tears through the onion-skin layers surrounding the sweet-smelling essence of *Melrose*. Character development? Bah! Continuity problems? Pooh-poohs! Real world parallels? Please!"

one with the audacity to step in the way of her success, anger is a dormant emotion for Heather.

"My sisters and I talk about how we suppress all our bad feelings, because we were taught to be nice girls," she revealed "We wouldn't speak up. In one of the first scenes I did on *Dynasty*, where I had to be angry, I started shaking and crying. And I thought, "Oh *this* is what happens when I get angry." I didn't know that. And it kind of freaked me out."

Heather still finds it difficult to deal with her anger, which

A MELROSE MOMENT
(AN EYE FOR AN EYE)

Amanda (brandishing a kitchen knife) to Jo and a bound peeping Tom caught spying on her through a hole in her bathroom and bedroom walls:

"You know, I've been sitting here all night trying to figure out what would make me feel better. And to see this pig dead would be a plus. But I'm not about to give up my life for his. I thought about jail. But it's just so—ordinary. Prisons are full of perverts, and you'd probably just make friends."

usually manifests itself as impatience or tears. "If I weren't an actress, I don't know where I would put all the anger and frustration. I'd probably have pimples all over my face. But I'd still be nice."

Fortunately for Heather, and her complexion, she's found an excellent outlet for her buried vexation—*Melrose Place.* "When she's in front of the TV camera and she gets to claw and scratch at people, that's how she gets out the frustrations that she has in everyday life," concluded Rob Tannenbaum, who profiled Heather for *Details.*

But unlike some celebrities who offer up their personal lives for public consumption, Heather is an intensely private person. Few have had access to her innermost thoughts. "I have a real hard time sharing my feelings," Heather confessed. "I can talk about everyone else about what's going on. But just don't ask me about my feelings."

She will admit, however, to feeling "socially inadequate," even as a seemingly well-adjusted adult. When I go to a party, I don't know what to say. I'm not really good with people I don't know."

And despite an ongoing struggle to build up her fragile self-esteem, Heather has learned what it means to assert herself. "I never used to be assertive, but now I can be," Heather declared recently. "I've been developing more of my male side. And I'm saying no really loud now. It's so funny—it used to be, 'Yes, yes,

Opposite: "I'm developing more of my male side."

136

whatever you want.' So now, when I do say no, I don't do it real tactfully. I'm like, 'NO!!' "

One of the things that has helped Heather feel better about herself is reaching out to those in need. In 1986, she signed up with the Youth Suicide Prevention Program after learning that her twenty-seven-year-old cousin Dale had shot and killed himself. Sadly it was not the first time that someone in her family had taken his own life. Ten years earlier, one of Heather's uncles, a struggling artist in his early thirties, had also shot and killed himself.

Since then, Heather has been plagued with a fear of losing a loved one. "I have a fear of a death in my family," she said. Although it was too late for Dale and her uncle, perhaps she could prevent someone else from making that fatal decision.

"You're never too busy for someone who needs you," she said of her work with the American Suicide Foundation. "All that really matters is being sensitive to someone's needs."

Another cause that Heather has embraced has been the plight of the homeless. In 1989, she led a march in Washington, D.C., to protest the government's laissez-faire attitude toward this issue. For the staunch Republican (she voted for Ronald Reagan twice), who had chosen not to particiapate in political demonstrations, even as a teenage rite of passage, the march was a unique and empowering experience.

"Heather can laugh at herself,'" Daphne said. "She knows what her image is."

When guys fantasize about sharing a bit of the bubbly with a woman, guess who they'd most like to rub-a-dub-dub. According to a 1994 Yardley Bath poll, 48 percent of the men who responded said Heather would put them in a lather.

Not that Heather is a man-stealer or anything—53 percent of the men selected their own wives or girlfriends. Heather's reaction: "Isn't it funny? A little popularity and people want to take a bath with you. Next year no one will want to be in my bathwater."

"I've never done anything like this before," she insisted, as she rallied in a celebrity caravan with Martin Sheen, Linda Evans, Carol Kane, Leslie Anne Warren, and Valerie Harper. "It felt so powerful with so many different rivers of people coming together. It's changed me, and I want to do all I can."

> ## "I've had sex on TV so many times I can't keep track."

She may be the ultimate knee-to-the-groin vixen on screen, but there is nothing hard-core about the real Heather Locklear. Nude scenes? Not likely. "I've never done a nude scene. It's pretty much out." And you will not find her undressed and unfolded within the pages of *Playboy* either.

In fact, the most risqué spreads she has done so far were for *Vanity Fair* and *Details,* where she posed respectively with legs akimbo and in rubber-and-lace lingerie.

How would she see herself in the role of Lady Macbeth? "Out, damned spot— I said out, goddammit!"

The truth is, despite her countless on-air lip-locks, Heather is more southern belle than Southern Cal in her modesty. "I've had sex on TV so many times I can't keep track," she said with a laugh. "I remember some good ones—but even the good ones are uncomfortable."

And should things get too steamy, there are always people who are paid to fill her fluffy mule slippers. "There was one movie I did where they used a body double," Heather recalled. "They [showed me] Polaroids of a bunch of girls in their bras. I looked them over and said, 'Okay, that one's good, that one looks a lot like me.'

"Emma Sams was in the movie with me and she said, 'Heather, you have to have them take their bras off because their boobs could fall down to their knees, and you don't want that to represent you!' So I looked at the pictures of the girls without their bras and I found one who I thought looked like me. When I saw the finished film, not only did [her breasts] not fall down, they didn't do anything. They just stayed right up there [pointing straight out in front of her], even when she was lying down!"

At thirty-three, Heather said she has never felt sexier, or been in better physical condition. The five-foot-five, 105-pound actress is, for the most part, a natural beauty. According to some reports the only trip she has made to the plastic surgeon (so far), has been for breast implants.

Although Heather continues to deny it, she reportedly got the augmentation at the request of then hubby Tommy. Apparently one of her breasts became infected after the operation, and she was put on heavy antibiotics. She was in a great deal of pain, a friend leaked to a reporter, and, for a while,

Emma Sams said, "Heather, you have to have them take their bras off because their boobs could fall down to their knees, and you don't want that to represent you!"

Those acting lessons have paid off after all. Heather was nominated for a 1994 Golden Globe Award by the Hollywood Foreign Press Association for best lead actress in a TV drama series. Her fellow honorees: Claire Danes (My So-Called Life), Jane Seymour (Dr. Quinn, Medicine Woman), Angela Lansbury (Murder, She Wrote), and Kathy Baker (Picket Fences).

Heather was nominated for a Golden Apple Award as one of the most newsworthy female stars of 1994. The other nominees in this category: Annette Bening, Julia Roberts, Meg Ryan, and Sharon Stone. The award, which went to Bening, was given by the Hollywood Women's Press Club at the Beverly Hilton Hotel in December. But that's okay—Heather had already received a Golden Apple Award as Discovery of the Year back in 1983.

Heather walked around with one breast larger than the other.

Her wounds eventually healed, and Heather now proudly displays her surgically enhanced cleavage in sexy, low-cut or sheer blouses. She gives her décollete an additional uplift by wearing the Wonderbra, which she buys in bulk from Bullock's in Los Angeles.

"I cannot live without these Wonderbras!" she told lingerie clerks while purchasing a dozen red, black, and white pushups. "I'd like to have them built into my clothing!"

Maintaining her flawless figure has never been a problem for Heather. If anything—and this is difficult for most women to hear—she's had to fight to keep the pounds on. Thus, her insatiable jones for high-fat, high-calorie junk food. "I don't diet," the featherweight actress revealed. "I try to gain weight by eating ice cream, hot dogs, and stuff."

In fact, she's been spotted at her favorite junk joint, Taco Bell, munching on burritos, chips, and salsa with her gal pals. "We just like to hang out and be girls," Heather said. "We just eat all the time."

Opposite: "I cannot live without these Wonderbras!"

Her favorite dish: tacos with extra cheese. She calls it "butt food," because she thinks the greasy grub makes a beeline for her butt.

As enviable as it sounds, being too thin has its own complications. When she was in her early twenties, Heather shrank to a mere ninety-four pounds after a tonsillectomy. She was finally able to regain the ten pounds she had lost by forcing herself to overeat for months.

"People often don't realize how hard it is for those who are underweight," Heather told a teen magazine shortly after her recovery. "You know that sick feeling you get after stuffing yourself with food? Well, that's how I feel all the time when

"People often don't realize how hard it is for those who are underweight."

I'm trying to gain weight. If I don't eat a good breakfast, lunch, and dinner, I'll lose."

Today, Heather stays in shape with the help of an eighty-dollar-an-hour personal trainer who supervises her daily routine of jumping rope, aerobics, and martial arts. In addition to her two- or three-hour workouts at the gym, the athletically inclined actress plays tennis, rides horseback, skis, bicycles, and indulges in her latest passion—golf.

And although Heather has never felt better about her body, she is keenly aware that beauty is fleeting, especially when you

"I don't use sex to get what I want. I get what I want first."
—Amanda

"Don't I recall something about you being on a honeymoon? Oh, I forgot, you have to get married in order to go on a honeymoon. So,

have your feet warmed up yet, or are they still cold?"
—Amanda to Alison

"If you're going to kiss me, don't do that pent-up macho anger thing. I don't like bruises."
—Amanda to Jake

are thrown, as she is, in the youth-engulfing maw of Hollywood. "I'm terrified of growing older," she confessed to a friend.

In the meantime, Heather flaunts her buffed-up bod on *Melrose* by wearing skin-tight suits with miniskirts; she has asked the wardrobe director to hike up her hemlines so her legs look longer. (If she could change anything about herself, the petite Heather said she would add three inches to her height.)

When she's not working her glamorous gams off, Heather prefers the casual comfort of jeans. At night Heather will wear an oversize T-shirt to bed, saving the sexy lingerie for special occasions such as Richie's return from the road. If she is sleeping solo, she will also slip a retainer into her mouth.

"I'm an attractive girl in my white T-shirt and retainer," she joked recently. "Here's the really scary part: I had to get my retainer refit, and they go, 'We've got this new thing where they glow in the dark.' So if I'm talking and the lights are off, you can see my gums moving."

One of her favorite beauty rituals is also a painful one: a do-it-yourself bikini wax: "I don't need it, but I do it for fun," she explains. "First of all—this is really disgusting—you have to let it grow out to a certain length, and after you get those, two days later there's other ones that have grown out to that certain length. You have to keep going back until it all evens out."

Heather stays in shape.

The Tenants of Melrose Place

If you're a single, gorgeous twenty- or thirtysomething man or woman, employed in a glam-job like advertising, you probably have the right stuff to rent an apartment in Amanda's unpretentious stucco complex.

When asked how much one of these fab apartments are going for these days, Heather replied, "I'm not sure. But you get to peek through the windows and sleep with the manager." (Actually, one episode quoted a one-bedroom going for a measly $800—not bad by L.A. standards.)

Of course, one of the current residents would have to move out or die first, which may be the case after last season's explosive final episode. In the meantime, here's at peek at the good, bad, but never ugly cast of characters and what Heather/Amanda thinks about them:

JAKE HANSON (GRANT SHOW): The brooding and somewhat dim blue-collar boy-toy who prefers the company of bikes, boats, and bimbos to that of other people. He was Jo's boyfriend until Amanda wormed her way into his heart. He worked briefly for Amanda's father, and his discovery of illegal activities landed Amanda's pop in jail (and nearly got Jake blown to bits).

HEATHER ON JAKE: "He's a <u>man.</u> That's what [Amanda] likes about him. He gives her a run for her money. That keeps her interested."

GRANT SHOW ON JAKE AND AMANDA: "I've always assumed that they had pretty good sex."

BILLY CAMPBELL (ANDREW SHUE): The pathetically p-whipped copywriter who was left at the altar by incest-suffering Alison. He has been called "a simpering blockhead" by some TV critics, for (among other things) moving to L.A. when Alison refused to live with him in New York. Has now found a new love in the *All About Eve* secretary, Brooke.

HEATHER ON BILLY: "Amanda loves Billy's playfulness, but he didn't satisfy her emotionally."

MATT FIELDING (DOUG SAVANT): *MP*'s gay social worker with a thing for men in uniform. He redefined the term "best man" at Billy and Alison's almost wedding. Aside from having the lamest part on the show, Matt is forever beholden to the evil Michael Mancini for doctoring the alcohol level in Michael's lab report after his car accident. Was last seen in jail falsely accused of murder—but who at *MP* hasn't been?

HEATHER ON TURNING MATT AROUND: "It's not really the kind of challenge Amanda is looking for."

MICHAEL MANCINI (THOMAS CALABRO): The duplicitous doctor who won't die, uses and abuses all his women, especially ex-wife Jane. He was blackmailed into marrying Jane's sister Sydney (she found out about the alcohol level in his blood test after his car crash), and no one ever shows up for any of his weddings. He is getting yet another divorce from psycho surgeon Kimberly, who stole Jo's baby after trying to run him over and asphyxiate him.

HEATHER ON MANCINI: "I think she'd have a good ol' time with Michael. The last time I told Thomas we should get together, he started running as fast as he could." (Michael and Amanda did join forces briefly during her bout with the big C.)

Jane Mancini (Josie Bissett): A struggling fashion entrepreneur, she is, above all, a loser at love. Sabotaged by her ex-hubby Michael, and rooked by her ex-business partner and fiancé, the Energizer Jane–Bunny just keeps getting dumped, and dumped and dumped and dumped.

AMANDA ON JANE: "What can I say—when God was passing

out business sense, Jane was in the back of the line getting her nails done."

SYDNEY ANDREWS (LAURA LEIGHTON): She's been a call girl, stripper, barmaid, and doctor's wife. The ever-scheming red-head has been rejected by nearly everyone (except for Jake and Jane's former fiancé, the embezzling Kangaroo-boy). Her desperation and verminlike survival skills are what make her character so wonderful to behold.

AMANDA TO SYDNEY, *after being released from prison:* "And to think your talents might have been wasted making license plates."

ALISON (COURTNEY THORNE-SMITH): Having flashbacks of incest with her father, Alison leaves Billy at the altar, loses her best friend, and winds up in rehab. As Amanda's underling, she is always at risk of being fired, demoted, or demeaned.

HEATHER ON ALISON: "You could say there's a kind of sexual tension between Amanda and Alison. I think Amanda wouldn't mind following up if she knew she could get a really good account."

COURTNEY ON HEATHER: "On *Melrose Place* I'm the proverbial victim—my part is the good girl. Heather gets to do *everything,* and I sit there and say, 'Ouch, ouch, ouch.'"

JO REYNOLDS (DAPHNE ZUNIGA): A fashion photographer from New York who carried a child for Reed and a torch for Jake. She kills Reed in self-defense and loses her baby (how many times?) to his Ozzie-and-Harriet-from-hell parents and then, again, to psycho doc Kimberly. She has the great distinction of being the only woman who Amanda befriends, and she even stood by Mandy's side during the peeping-Tom incident.

AMANDA TO JO: "Stay out of this, Jo."

MELROSE, B.A. (BEFORE AMANDA)

Yes, there was life in Melrose before Amanda. It came in the form of **VANESSA WILLIAMS,** (the rental's only African-American resident), who played the energetic aerobics instructor Rhonda, and **AMY LOCANE,** who played the starlet Sandy. By late fall of 1992, Sandy was replaced by Jo, and Rhonda was written out during the 1993–94 season.

From Miniskirt to Miniseries

After the second season's cliff-hanging episode was put to bed last summer, Heather immediately signed on to do *Texas Justice*. The four-hour ABC minseries based on the book *Blood Will Tell*, aired on February 12–13, 1995 .In it, she plays Priscilla, the wife of T. Cullen Davis (Peter Straus), known as the richest American ever tried for murder.

When the movie begins, Cullen and Priscilla are having an affair. The two get married, she moves into the estate, and the marriage starts to fall apart. At first, he drinks too much and is insanely jealous. But soon he tires of her and asks for a divorce. Priscilla refuses, hating to leave the lavish lifestyle to which she had become accustomed. Set in the swinging seventies, the movie features a sexually promiscuous Priscilla throwing wild parties and having several affairs with some hunky hangers-on.

> *"I have to be sexual toward a lot of people, which I probably shouldn't be."*

"She doesn't have a mean bone in her pretty little body."
—Dennis Franz

Heather was named one of *Entertainment Weekly's* "1994 Entertainers of the Year." Topping out at number 4, the magazine gushed, *"Melrose's* sly fox has killer legs—and so does her career." Joining Heather on *EW's* A list: Tom Hanks, Tim Allen, Quentin Tarantino, Jim Carrey, Michael Crichton, Hugh Grant, Ricki Lake, Boyz II Men, Dennis Franz, Brett Butler, and Trent Reznor.

One night a masked gunman breaks into the manse, killing her young daughter and permanently wounding Priscilla. She charges Cullen with orchestrating a plot to murder her, and he is eventually brought to trial.

"It's a true story about justice that hasn't been served well," Heather explained. "My husband, who is a trillionaire, tries to divorce me, and the proceedings take so long that he shoots me. He doesn't kill me, but he kills my daughter and my boyfriend—and he gets off."

Cullen is exonerated despite the fact that an unsympathetic judge is conveniently assassinated, and a hit list with fifteen names on it is uncovered during an FBI sting operation.

What does Heather think of the real-life Priscilla, whom many dismissed as "trailer trash" when compared to the lofty Cullen? "[Priscilla] is a good person—she loves her kid," she said, "but she's definitely a party girl. She likes attention. She likes to be the center of it and she likes to get a reaction, especially from men. . . . She likes to go out and party all night. Or stay in and party—like when she and her boyfriend allegedly swapped partners with another couple."

To get that attention, party-girl Priscilla would drape herself in red sequined gowns with plunging necklines and flashy jewelry. "I would be hiding in a corner wearing a high-neck dress," gasped Heather, comparing herself to Priscilla. "I don't usually show off as much as this character, and I have to be sexual toward a lot of people, which I probably shouldn't be. I can't wait to get done with this and get back to normal."

Her Heatherness called the offer "sweet," but did not accept, much to the morning radio host's eternal disappointment.

Although TV critics were divided in their opinion of the movie, they were unanimous in their praise for Heather's performance. John Podhoretz of the *New York Post* said it was a role that Heather was "born and aerobicized to play"; and *Newsday's* TV critic Diane Werts wrote, "Locklear works her way under Priscilla's skin and fleshes the script's clichés out into a real, live woman with a lot going on inside her."

HEATHER'S UNCHARITABLE REBUFF

When Heather was in Austin filming the ABC miniseries *Texas Justice,* lovesick KLBJ deejay Bob Fonseca promised to donate $500 to a listener's favorite charity if he or she could convince Heather to appear in-studio. Fonseca has been a fan since *The Return of Swamp Thing.* Her Heatherness called the offer "sweet," but did not accept, much to the morning radio host's eternal disappointment.

In its year-end tribute, *US* magazine cited Heather as one of "The 94 Biggest Stories of '94." Praised the entertainment mag: "The driving force behind the villains and vamps of *Melrose Place*. She's so good at saving sinking ships, the folks at *Saturday Night Live* should take notice."

The national *Entertainment Weekly* gushed: "Leave it to Heather Locklear to remind us why the long-form made-for-television movie was invented. Locklear is an ideal television actress who excels at mean-minded melodrama. She may not have the glamorous richness of a movie star, but she deploys the sort of sexy superficiality that comes across on the small screen as both excitingly realistic and giddily exaggerated. She is what is commonly called a hoot."

And, like her *Melrose* costars, the cast and crew members of *Texas Justice* had only the nicest things to say about the series' star. "She doesn't have a mean bone in her pretty little body," observed costar Dennis Franz of *NYPD Blue,* who played Cullen's flamboyant defense attorney Richard "Racehorse" Haynes.

"She's a doll." "No big ego." "No moody temperament," others

Entertainment Weekly gushed, "Melrose's sly fox has killer legs—and so does her career."

commented. And according to author Gary Cartwright, she even got Priscilla's limp down pat.

Although the heat was unbearable in Austin, Texas, where the movie was being filmed, Heather bore it all with her usual good humor. To help cool things down, a generator pumped cold air through a huge centipedelike tube for the outdoor scenes. "It's supposed to be for inside, but we won't tell anyone," Heather whispered gratefully to a reporter on the set.

As she spoke, Peter Straus sneaked up behind her and kissed her playfully on the neck. "It's like being on *Melrose Place*," he joked between nibbles. "Oh, honey, oh, honey, I'm sorry! She was in my room, she had the wrong key. . ."

Heather giggled with delight. "Isn't this fun? This is what I'm doing on my hiatus. I couldn't ask for anything better."

About her sexy, champagne-soaked love scene with Straus: "If I really got turned on, I'd feel uncomfortable and self-conscious," she said. "It wouldn't work. I don't want to think that it's *me* there. . ."

Actor Greg Michaels, who played Priscilla's boyfriend Woody, remembered how Heather helped him pull a prank on an old friend who visited him on location. "My friend Bill from Houston always teases me about meeting starlets," Greg said. "So I told Heather's makeup lady, Lisa, to ask him about his nickname 'Handsome Bill.' "I never even spoke to Heather about it."

A few hours later, Greg and Bill walked into Heather's trailer. "Are you from Houston?" Heather asked the startled Bill. "Was your nickname Handsome Bill?" she continued playfully, watching him turn various shades of red.

"She did it so straight-faced, that she even had me going for a while," Greg recalled. "Bill went gaga, thinking that Heather Locklear knew about his nickname and reputation."

Greg said the script called for him to do several "orgy scenes" with Heather. In one scene, Woody and Priscilla swap partners and start making love to other people. In another flashback scene, the script indicated that Woody and Priscilla should "frolic."

"Heather and I kidded each other about what we should do when we 'frolic,'" Greg recalled. "They were supposed to shoot the scene in the bedroom, then they changed it to the bathroom tub, and then they changed it again to a hot tub outdoors. It ended up being Heather sunning herself by the pool and me popping up out of the water to give her a little kiss on the stomach. That was it."

The so-called "orgy" scene was equally tame. "There were about ten people piled into an r.v., drinking and doing drugs," as Greg described it. "Heather and I wander back to the bedroom, and a girl starts taking off her blouse. Heather and I start kissing, and the camera cuts away. Not much of an orgy really. But every guy on the set asked me if he could be my body double."

Despite appearances, Heather's heart belonged solely to Richie, who heated things up even more on the weekends by flying down from Jersey to be with her. And when he couldn't break away from his musical commitments, Heather would hop a plane to see him. "Any free time I had I was with my husband," she said, "so I had lots and lots and lots of fun." This

She's definitely a party girl. She likes attention. She likes to be the center of it and she likes to get a good reaction, especially from men.

went on until July, when she returned to L.A. to start the next season's *Melrose.*

HEATHER IS WORST DRESSED

Everyone's a critic. Especially Mr. Blackwell, the king of sartorial sarcasm, who included Heather in his thirty-fifth annual list of "Worst-Dressed Women." Her fashion folly, according to Blackwell: "From a Spandex siren, to a latex Lolita, a tribute to design dementia."

Blackwell is not alone, however, in his disdain for Heather's duds. *The Star*, which features celebrity's most horrific get-ups each week, described Heather when captured by a photographer wearing a black, see-through number, looking "like the main attraction at a burlesque show."

PILOGUE
Our Landlady of
Melrose Place

At this writing, Heather is entering a new stage in her personal life and career. She may finally achieve her dream of becoming a full-fledged movie star. In February of 1994, she was offered the lead in a Universal black comedy called *Intolerable Cruelty.* The feature film, about a greedy divorcing couple, will be written and directed by Joel and Ethan Coen, whose impressive credits include *Blood Simple, Raising Arizona,* and *Miller's Crossing,* and is scheduled to begin production during her next hiatus from *Melrose.*

Heather is also being considered for an action picture from producers Joel Silver and David Geffen called *Executive Decisions.* It costars veteran film actor Kurt Russell.

And if she fails to launch yet another film career, she could always host her own TV talk show. "I've always thought, 'Wow! What a great job to be on TV with a talk show like Regis and Kathie Lee!,' " she told a *TV Guide* reporter. "They sit there, chat about the day, interview a guest. When I hosted *Saturday Night Live,* I was Lila Klein, on 'Coffee Talk.' [New York accent] 'It's neither a thigh nor a master—discuss.' "

On the home front, she and Richie currently spend much of their time at Heather's $3.4 million San Fernando villa with a brood of two rottweilers, a Yorkie named Kitty and two Maltese terriers.

The 7,400-square-foot estate, which she decorated herself, has a gourmet kitchen, wine cellar, formal dining room, pool,

Mondays are a bitch.
MP
MELROSE PLACE MOVES TO MONDAYS
Season Premiere September 12 • 8PM/7PM Central & Mountain
FOX

patio, barbecue, and waterfall. Heather and Richie can soak in the breathtaking mountain view from the sauna or whirlpool, or spend intimate evenings in front of the fireplace in the family room. There are even "his" and "hers" showers in the bathroom.

Of course, Heather's parents live just minutes away, so her dad can drop by for a cappuccino in the mornings before heading off to work. And whenever she is feeling lonely (i.e., Richie is away), she will invite her folks over to keep her company in the evenings.

"They help keep me grounded because I live so close to them," she says. "If I were from Iowa or something and my parents didn't know what I was doing, I could get lost in a certain type of lifestyle."

And speaking of neighborhoods—*Melrose Place* is nearing the end of its third year as the hottest address on Fox Network. In this past season:

—Kimberly has come back from the dead to haunt Michael, snatch away Jo's baby, attempt suicide, join a "Victims No More" group, and blow up *Melrose Place.*

—Sydney is arrested for attempted murder, sprung from a mental institution, blackmailed into having sex with her sister

Heather never regained her footing after this disastrous beginning.

On December 7, 1994, Heather cohosted the annual Billboard Music Awards with actor-comedian Dennis Miller. With the possible exception of the winners, this was not a memorable evening for anyone involved.

Visibly uncomfortable, Heather was barely audible over the cheering rock fans pressed against the stage inside L.A.'s Universal Amphitheater. She said "good evening" no less than five times before the crowd finally quieted down.

Putting the fans up front, the thinking goes, recreates the excitement of a rock concert—a missing element when the seats are warmed by the perpetually bored bottoms of music executives. In the case of the Billboard Awards, this arrangement created the atmosphere of a high school pep rally.

Heather and Dennis's opening monologue was completely ignored by the frenzied fans, still pumped by the earsplitting opening act. Heather never regained her footing after this disastrous beginning. She spent the remainder of the show swallowing, droning, or tripping amateurishly over her lines.

BEST MOMENTS: When Heather first appeared on stage. She looked stunning in a see-through black shirt with a satin bra and silk bolero jacket by the Italian designer team Domenico Dolce and Stefano Gabbana. The midriff-exposing outfit inspired the best line of the evening, ad libbed by Dennis Miller: "I knew you were an inny." Heather later changed into a sexy black slip dress with a feathery hem.

Weirdest moments: William Shatner plugging his next project while presenting the Country Artist Award; the Rolling Stones, via satellite, who got up and left their award on the table after their chat with Dennis was over; and a bloated Billy Joel accepting an award from Sydney, Australia.

Over the years, Heather has tried on many personas for her various TV and film roles. And for every part she has played, she has sported a certain "look," befitting the times and Heather of the moment.

As the squeaky clean Stacy on *T. J. Hooker* (1982–87), Heather wore schoolgirl bangs and ponytail. As the trampy Sammy Jo on *Dynasty,* her blond locks were teased and frosted into a frenzied 'do. Today, in her mature role as Amanda, Heather has turned to hairstylist Masood of the famous Institute de Beauté in Los Angeles to get the power-exec look of the nineties.

Masood encouraged her to abandon her tough-girl tresses and adopt a softer, more sensuous style. "When Heather came to me a year ago, her hair was all one length, and she hated it," he said. "We did soft, long layers to give her hair body and swing. The look is very versatile for a nineties woman and is simple to style. It lets her be a little adventurous with her hairdos without making a permanent change."

And since Amanda is not one to fade demurely into the background, Heather has decided that being bolder than ever means being blonder than ever. "I went to some other colorists and they said, 'Oh no, you can't go that light,' " Heather said. "But I wanted it lighter; now I stand out more, rather than looking mousey."

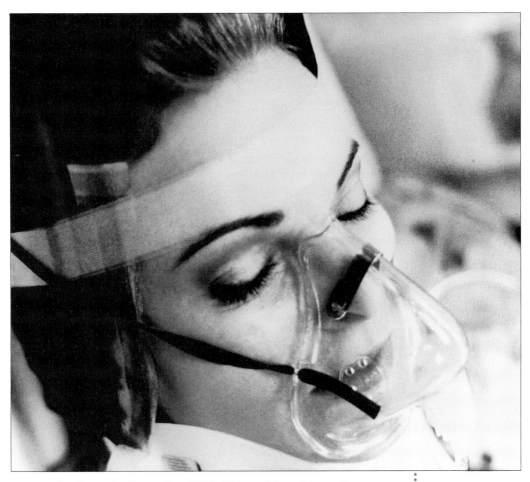

Heather under the weather. Will Hodgkins end Amanda's reign?

Jane's evil ex-fiancé from down under, and given a job as wait-ress at Shooters.

—Jake escapes death on the high seas, has a fling with Sydney, sleeps with Jo, becomes owner of Shooters, and is reunited with his bad-boy brother.

—Alison loses Billy to her best friend, and then, again, to her secretary, drowns her sorrows in the bottle, goes into rehab, has a fling with a sexoholic, takes over as president of D&D, and is dethroned by Amanda.

—Amanda is robbed and deserted by her father; two-timed

HEATHER IS MOST LOVABLE

When *TV Guide* surveyed Hollywood insiders about the most lovable TV stars, Heather scored a whopping 93 on the tube bible's 1994 "lovability index." She took fourth place directly behind *Murder She Wrote's* beloved sleuth Angela Lansbury.

Quoth the *Guide:* "Blond, beautiful, and playing a vixen on *Melrose Place,* she should be that word that rhymes with witch. But Locklear has a stunningly down-to-earth side. . . . Either she's found inner peace or she's taking too much Valium." Heather got an additional honorable mention for being bearer of the best gift of the year; she gave long, plush terrycloth bathrobes to everyone on the set.

Opposite: The tenants of Melrose Place. Back row: Matt Fielding, Jake Hanson, Michael Mancini. Front row: Jo Reynolds, Alison Parker, Amanda Woodward, Billy Campbell, Jane Mancini.

"If I were from Iowa or something and my parents didn't know what I was doing, I could get lost in a certain type of lifestyle."

Heather, Lorretta Young and Tom Selleck.

HOLY COW

What do Heather, Tori Spelling, Christie Brinkley, and En Vogue have in common? They have all agreed to pose with milk mustaches for the Milk Foundation's new ad campaign. Each milk model will reportedly receive $25,000 for her pains. This will be Heather's second endorsement for the milky way.

and nearly killed by a drop-dead gorgeous doctor whose ambitions and libido actually surpass her own; fired from D&D only to return as the boss and then get fired again, survives a bout with cancer, and is pursued by the maniacal Michael Mancini.

By the time you read this, these problems will have been solved and replaced by new ones. Perhaps more will have "died" and come back to life. New characters will have come and gone. And if popular culture continues to define the decades, *Melrose Place* and Heather Locklear will go down in history as the undisputed phenoms of the nineties.

HEATHER IS MOST INTRIGUING

In *3* magazine's annual best-and worst-of roundup, Heather was selected one of "The 25 Most Intriguing People of 1994." The celebrity mag said, "the cold, imperious snap of her character's voice could have cowed Queen Victoria." Joining her on the I-list: Bill Clinton, Newt Gingrich, Tim Allen, Jim Carrey, John Travolta, O. J. Simpson, Princess Diana, and the Pope.

Heather was also named one of "The 25 Most Fascinating Women of 1994" by *Ladies' Home Journal,* along with the likes of California prosecutor Marcia Clark, Lisa Marie Presley-Jackson, Oprah Winfrey, Reba McEntire, Glenn Close, and Diane Sawyer.

Phew, what a year!

At 33, Heather says she has
never felt sexier.